TEACHING INTRODUCTORY PSYCHOLOGY

SURVIVAL TIPS FROM THE EXPERTS

EDITED BY

ROBERT J. STERNBERG

AMERICAN PSYCHOLOGICAL ASSOCIATION
WASHINGTON, DC

Published by
American Psychological Association
750 First Street, NE
Washington, DC 20002

Copies may be ordered from
APA Order Department
P.O. Box 92984
Washington, DC 20090-2984

In the United Kingdom and Europe, copies may be ordered from
American Psychological Association
3 Henrietta Street
Covent Garden
London WC2E 8LU
England

Typeset in Meridien by Harlowe Typography, Inc., Cottage City, MD

Printer: Braun-Brumfield, Ann Arbor, MI
Jacket designer: Minker Design, Bethesda, MD
Technical/production editor: Tanya Y. Alexander

Library of Congress Cataloging-in-Publication Data
Teaching introductory psychology : survival tips from the experts /
  Robert J. Sternberg, editor.
      p.   cm.
  Includes bibliographical references and index.
  ISBN 1-55798-417-4 (pbk.)
  1. Psychology—Study and teaching (Higher)   I. Sternberg, Robert
J.
  BF77.T42   1997
  150'.71'1—dc21   97-3870
                                                         CIP

British Library Cataloguing-in-Publication Data
A CIP record is available from the British Library.

Printed in the United States of America
First edition

This book is dedicated to
Robert G. Crowder,
who has motivated and influenced me
in more ways than he knows.

Contents

Contributors

Douglas A. Bernstein, University of Illinois, Urbana–Champaign

Charles L. Brewer, Furman University

Peter Gray, Boston College

Richard A. Griggs, University of Florida

Lester A. Lefton, University of South Carolina

Margaret W. Matlin, State University of New York, Geneseo

Charles G. Morris, University of Michigan

David G. Myers, Hope College

Rod Plotnik, San Diego State University

Joshua M. Smyth, State University of New York, Stony Brook

Robert J. Sternberg, Yale University

Carole E. Wade, Dominican College of San Rafael

Camille B. Wortman, State University of New York, Stony Brook

Philip G. Zimbardo, Stanford University

Preface

Ten years after I had taken the introductory psychology course as a college freshman, I was teaching it. Looking at my students' blank gazes staring back at me, I wondered whether some of them were not soon going to be looking for other majors. I wasn't really reaching the students: I needed help. This book is intended to provide the help that I needed and that many and perhaps most instructors of introductory psychology can also use.

When I taught introductory psychology for the first time, I was determined not to make what I thought was the biggest mistake my introductory psychology teacher had made. He had taught the course primarily for someone else—for someone who learns well by memory. I don't. I learn better when there are lots of creative activities. So I taught the course that I would have loved to have taken. But in doing so, I made the same mistake my teacher had made. I taught for just one type of student—in this case, those who learned the way I did. I now try to teach for all kinds of learners. Reading this book will help teachers of introductory psychology reach all of the types of learners in their classrooms.

The help comes from those who probably best know the introductory psychology course: seasoned instructors who not only have taught the course for many years but also have written their own widely selling introductory psychology textbooks. Few individuals have thought as long and as deeply about the introductory psychology course as have its textbook writers. They *have to* have given the course much thought: Writing an introductory psychology text was a monumental undertaking for me, one that dwarfed even my (more than 850-page) doctoral dissertation. It is not a task for the faint-hearted or the weary. And there is always the probability—and a fairly substantial one—that the text will be stillborn and die before it even sells out its first printing. Writing a textbook, therefore, requires not only that the author think deeply about the course but also that he or she come up with some new and exciting ideas about how to teach it.

When I have compared introductory psychology texts and thought about which to use and how to use them in my own course, I have often wondered what the authors might have to say about how most effectively to teach the course. What I found myself wanting was not quite an instructor's manual—which can be quite long and which the text authors usually do not write in any case—but a pithy statement of the authors' philosophy of the course as well as of how they would motivate and engage students in its content. Especially as a beginning teacher, but even now as an experienced teacher, I have thought that I could profit from the collective wisdom of those who have thought about and taught the course for many years. This book provides that wisdom.

My goal in editing this book was to invite authors to articulate their philosophies, course designs, and teaching techniques for the introductory psychology course. I requested chapters that were conceptually sound but also practically useful. I told authors to write a chapter for all introductory psychology teachers and to address how the teaching of introductory psychology could be made more rewarding to students and teachers alike. A few authors comment specifically on the writing process of introductory textbooks, and the parallels they have found between the classes they teach and the material they write. I hope these chapters help to shed light on any introductory textbook's underlying purpose, goals, and organization and thus enable teachers to use these essential texts more effectively.

I am happy to say that 11 authors of successful introductory psychology texts have contributed to this volume: Douglas A. Bernstein, Peter Gray, Lester A. Lefton, Margaret W. Matlin, Charles G. Morris, David G. Myers, Rod Plotnik, Carole E. Wade, Camille B. Wortman (with collaborator Joshua Smyth), Philip G. Zimbardo, and myself. All of these authors have taught introductory psychology many times.

The authors represent great diversity: Some teach in large universities; others, in small colleges. Some have written longer books; others, shorter books. Some have written texts that are considered relatively upper level; others, texts that are considered relatively lower level. Some have written texts with a more natural science orientation; others, texts with a more social science orientation. What they have in common is a passion for teaching introductory psychology and the experience to match.

I am pleased also to say that there are two additional chapters—a prologue and an epilogue—by award-winning teachers of introductory psychology who have not written introductory textbooks—Richard A. Griggs and Charles L. Brewer. I chose these individuals for their experience in the field and for their ability to give a broad overview of the chapters that is representative of a perspective somewhat different from that of a textbook author.

This is a book for any teacher of the introductory psychology course. Those who teach other courses in psychology may find it quite useful as well. Indeed, I suspect that much of what is said here would be useful to any college teacher, because so many of the principles of good teaching apply across disciplines. I have myself taught introductory psychology many times, but I can honestly say that I have learned a great deal from my reading of the teaching philosophies and techniques of the other teachers presented in this book.

I am grateful to Susan Reynolds for contracting the book, to Julia Frank-McNeil for continuing the editing work on the book, and to Peggy Schlegel for finishing the editing work on the book. Beth Beisel was an outstanding development editor. I am grateful also to some of the truly outstanding undergraduate psychology teachers I had—Bob Abelson for statistics, Jay Braun for physiological psychology, Bob Crowder for information-processing psychology, Bill Kessen for child psychology, Arnold Lazarus for abnormal psychology, Endel Tulving for the psychology of memory, and Alex Wearing for the psychology of thinking—for their influence on me. And I am grateful to my children, Seth and Sara Sternberg, who proved that members of the Sternberg family can get an *A* in an introductory psychology course.

Richard A. Griggs

Prologue

Teaching introductory psychology may be the most intellectually challenging of all our scholarly activities.

GRAY, p. 50

What greater life mission could one hope for than to do one's part to restrain intuition with critical thinking, judgmentalism with compassion, and illusion with understanding?

MYERS, p. 109

These quotes from 2 of the 11 chapters in this volume summarize the challenge and the reward of teaching introductory psychology. For those of us who teach this course, both of these aspects are clear. It is a continual challenge to teach this course well. I have taught over 50 sections of the introductory course, but I still find myself searching for a better way. I keep coming back to the same basic questions that we must all answer. What are my most important objectives for this course? How can I best meet these objectives? Which chapters should I assign? Which topics should I lecture on? How much should I lecture? How many demonstrations and class activities should I include? Have I been successful in getting my students to think more critically, more scientifically? And the list goes on. The reward, however, when one does succeed is overwhelming; but these peak experiences are too few and far between for most of us. We would like to do a better job. We would like to have more positive experiences. That's the rub—how to achieve this. Where can we turn for ideas? Why not to the textbook writers? Surely, given their experience both teaching the course and writing the texts for the course, they have confronted such questions and developed answers, their philosophies for teaching this course. This was Bob Sternberg's idea, and the 11 responses to his request for these philosophies constitute this unique volume.[1]

So what will one find in these 11 chapters? Just as the Tables of Contents of the authors' texts look very similar but the actual texts are very different, so too is it that in this volume common issues are confronted but answered in very different ways; but this variance is important and will stimulate your thinking about your own philosophy for teaching the introductory psychology course. In the remainder of this prologue, I provide a few examples of the issues discussed herein.

The texts have become so encyclopedic, I can't cover everything. I only have one term to teach the course. Which chapters should I assign? How many should I assign? Wade summarizes this best, "Faced with 10 zillion studies and 3 thousand theories, and only one semester (usually) to teach them, teachers and textbook authors must be selective" (p. 159). All introductory psychology teachers face this problem, and all of us resolve it in our own way, as do the textbook authors. For example, Bernstein assigns and tests on the entire text because he thinks that students are responsible adults whose task it is to learn textbook material whether he lectures on it or not. Consider Morris, who says that the textbook is the core of his introductory course and that he makes it clear to students that he expects them to master the content of the text. Or consider Gray's idea that introductory psychology instructors become "slaves to the textbook." In his words,

> Many assume they must cover in lectures everything they assign in the textbook or it is not fair game on the test; conversely, many assume that nothing said in lectures is fair game unless it also appears in the book. A great liberation occurs when the instructor realizes that both of these assumptions are false. (p. 55)

I would be remiss, however, if I did not point out the importance of placing these authors' comments within their appropriate contexts. One needs to know an individual's entire philosophy before judging only one aspect of it. For example, one needs to know what these teachers do in class, another set of questions teachers must confront.

How do I use lecture time? Should I lecture and cover as much of the information as possible in my one term? What topics should I lecture on? Should I incorporate activities and demonstrations into my classes? Am I wasting valu-

---

[1]Excellent articles on teaching introductory psychology by two more introductory psychology textbook authors already exist (Gleitman, 1984; McConnell, 1978), and I highly recommend them. They nicely complement the present volume.

able class time if I do this? Here again the answers are varied. For example, Wortman and Smyth argue that instead of offering lectures on the major topics covered in the textbooks, teachers should supplement the textbook by lecturing only on topics they feel passionate about teaching. In their view, when a teacher conveys passion for a topic, interest is more likely to be evoked in the students. My favorite on this topic is Gray's "idea-centered" approach to teaching the introductory course. Rather than focus on facts, terms, and topics in the textbook, this approach focuses explicitly on important ideas as the subject matter of the course. Gray provides us with an excellent description of the elements of such a course, from giving the idea-based lecture to helping students meet the challenge of such a course. This is an example of liberal arts teaching at its best, and I highly recommend it for those of you with this bent.

With respect to the use of class activities and demonstrations, many of the authors strongly favor their use, and some actually provide descriptions of a few of their own. For example, Zimbardo says that the "Don't tell me, show me" principle is the one by which his lectures live, and he proceeds to give us several excellent examples of demonstrations he has conducted in his classrooms on both animal and human behavior. Plotnik also provides interesting and valuable information on class activities, especially for new teachers.

In addition to these content and class activity questions, the authors spend a large chunk of time on an objective most (if not all) of us pursue—that of developing students' critical thinking skills. It is certainly an objective of our introductory psychology textbooks. Anyone examining many of these texts would easily deduce this fact. Thus, it is not very surprising that it forms a part of these textbook authors' philosophies. We especially see it in Wade's chapter, as she and Carol Tavris essentially defined it for the introductory textbook market in the first edition of their introductory text. We expect that Sternberg's chapter will be organized around his triarchic theory of thinking and intelligence, as are his recent texts in both introductory and cognitive psychology, and it is. Both Wade and Sternberg focus on getting students to think "like psychologists," a goal of many introductory psychology teachers.

As with critical thinking, diversity is another issue that seems crucial for introductory textbooks and teachers to confront, and our authors do so. In this case, Matlin is noteworthy, with her section on addressing diversity in introductory psychology. Given its autobiographical nature (e.g., her family's work with preschoolers in Nicaragua), her commentary is especially fascinating.

Also in this volume are several discussions of the parallels between the authors' classroom teaching and textbook writing (teaching in the broader sense) philosophies. Lefton's chapter is a prominent example. Myers and Matlin also provide us with such discussions, in addition to information on the writing process. Myers's chapter, for example, has two unique sections—one on how teachers' values guide their teaching and writing and another on responses to questions about writing and publishing.

Several authors also include discussions of their motivations for writing their texts. Matlin is a notable example. In her own words, "In summary, a major motivator for my decision to write an introductory psychology textbook was to understand more about the Big Picture, to try to fit together some new pieces into the jigsaw puzzle" (p. 75). For others, the type of text that they wanted was not available, so they wrote their own text.

Most of the questions and issues that I have mentioned are those that one would expect in a book such as this; but does this book provide any unexpected information? To some extent, the answer is yes. For the most part, this information is pragmatic. Plotnik's chapter will be valuable to those of us who train and supervise inexperienced graduate student instructors of introductory psychology. In it, he describes his experiences as supervisor of his department's teaching assistants and the three-component model he has developed for effective teaching of the introductory course. One will also find some interesting ideas about the use of undergraduate students as teaching assistants for the introductory course. Wortman and Smyth's and Gray's chapters provide this information.

In summary, what one will find in this volume are the philosophies of 11 introductory textbook authors for teaching the introductory course, a mixed bag of ideas with which to contrast our own ideas about teaching this course. They also allow us a better understanding of each author as teacher or as textbook writer; some even permit a glimpse of the author's personality. One will find two of these prominent authors still ruminating about getting Cs in their introductory courses as undergraduates. The implications of this behavior are left for the reader to contemplate. I was particularly impressed by Myers's obvious passion for teaching and writing and his discussion of some early, very unfavorable criticism of the first edition of his introductory text. First, it was difficult for me to believe that anyone who had actually reviewed his excellent text could tender such criticism; but it is his advice for dealing with such criticism that stays with me. Briefly, Myers advises, "If after pondering the criticism, you retain a vision, hold to it. Keep your eye on the goal" (p. 116). This also seems to be good advice for all of us as we strive to make our introductory courses the best they can be. We can take advice from others about teaching this course, and as in this book, we can read the philosophies of others for teaching this course. Each of us, however, has our own vision for the course; and although we should consider the thoughts of others, we should remember that it is our course and we should keep *our vision*.

References

Gleitman, H. (1984). Introducing psychology. *American Psychologist, 39,* 421–427.

McConnell, J. V. (1978). Confessions of a textbook writer. *American Psychologist, 33,* 159–169.

Philip G. Zimbardo

A Passion for Psychology:

Teaching It Charismatically, Integrating Teaching and Research Synergistically, and Writing About It Engagingly

1

I began teaching introductory psychology to a small class at Yale University in 1957 as the first graduate student in the psychology department ever given the privilege of teaching the rare breed of "Yale man" of that era. Having taken Chairperson Claude Buxton's course in The Teaching of Psychology, I was prepared (and begged) to teach one of the many sections of Psychology 101 when a professor was unable to do so. Since that time some 40 years ago, I have taught this course regularly to small honors classes, to large lecture classes numbering up to 750 students, and to all of the in-between sizes and shapes of students at Yale, at New York University (NYU), and at Stanford University since 1968.

My Teaching Background

When I arrived at NYU as the only assistant professor in the psychology department's Bronx campus, my small band of senior colleagues were only too happy to dump on me a rather heavy teaching and advising load. Thus, I ended up teaching introductory psychology as many as three times every year (three consecutive semesters, including summer school) within a horrendous course load of 13 semester courses (5 each term, 2 in summer school, and 1 extra moonlighting venture at Yale College or Barnard College to make ends nearly meet while surviving in New York City on a lowly assistant professor's stipend). In the process, I learned a lot of psychology and somehow managed to sustain a love for general psychology despite the intense work that this unique course load demanded. Some might invoke a dissonance theory explanation, but Daryl Bem's self-perception principle would serve equally well, to account for this love of what you perceive you are suffering for.

However, for someone equally enamored of experimental research as of teaching, I had to discover survival tactics to "cheat" my enemy—time—by creating a synergy, rather than an opposition, between teaching efforts and research efforts. I had to figure out how to use teaching as a vehicle for getting research ideas and then to recycle my research back into new and better teaching. We'll return to this theme of professionally viable cheating toward the end of this chapter.

I should start out by confessing that I did not always love psychology; indeed, there was a time during my undergraduate days at Brooklyn College when I hated psychology! I was convinced that it was a chaotic, uninspiring field wherein researchers asked rather trivial questions and went to great lengths with precise methods to come up with only probable answers. Did I mention that I got a *C* grade in my introductory psychology course at Brooklyn College—my only *C* among a hotshot summa cum laude record? The teaching was so poor, and the text so boring, that I immediately switched my prospective major from psychology to sociology/anthropology. Unfortunately, I later found that sociologists asked grand questions but rarely came up with any convincing answers. I switched back to psychology in my senior year after taking an exciting course in experimental psychology. So perhaps one must entertain the hypothesis that all of my concern for effective teaching and inspired writing about psychology is merely an attempt to undo the situational variables to which I attribute my poor outcome in that first formal introduction to psychology. Surely, I, as a card-carrying "situationist" (bred from the same environmental influences as my high school classmate Stanley Milgram), would be the last to endorse a dispositional explanation for this personal anomaly.

Beginning Near the End: Status Matters

I'd like to begin peeling away at the core of this chapter by sharing a story of how a recent teaching triumph turned into a near disaster but was rescued through serendipitous insight into a quirk in my teaching style of which I had been unaware in all my many years of teaching. Then I go on to discuss my philosophy for teaching introductory psychology, backed up by specific strategies and tactics I use to achieve my fundamental goal: to make psychology memorable by teaching charismatically. After outlining how I created a synergy between my teaching and my research, I conclude by briefly summarizing how textbooks in psychology have an impact on the teaching of psychology. I note in particular how *Psychology and Life* has had a revolutionary impact on the teaching and textbook writing of psychology because of the innovations introduced by its originator, Floyd Ruch, back in 1937.

LECTURERS VERSUS TV ANCHORS

After being notified by Boston station WGBH that I was a finalist in the search for a narrator and scientific advisor of their projected series on introductory psychology, I had to arrange to give several lectures on the East Coast so that their staff could evaluate me up close. Barry Schwartz, the chair at Swarthmore, and one of the small band of outstanding undergraduates from my NYU days, invited me to give two lectures to various groups of those typically intense Swarthmore students. The lectures were on long-term interests of mine, shyness and the psychology of evil, embellished with vivid slides guaranteed to elicit audience interest. The lively discussion afterward was just what the Boston folks had hoped to see, and they hired me on the spot to front the 26-program public television series *Discovering Psychology*. After I wrote the grant proposal for the psychological content and organizational aspects of the series (that the Annenberg/CPB—Corporation for Public Broadcasting—project finally funded), we were ready to shoot.

The general format of the programs was for my introductory statement to set the theme of the program, followed by relevant archival footage, interviews with significant contributors to each major area of psychology, and re-creations or demonstrations of important experiments. Between each of these program elements, I would appear in various settings—classrooms, clinics, hospitals, city streets, forests, and more—to provide continuity, and then offer some concluding commentary that would link each program to the next in the series. But after the first week of shooting at Stanford University, word came back from the East Coast producers that it just wasn't working. I was somehow all wrong, what they saw at the Swarthmore lectures was not what I was delivering to the TV cameras. My part of the West Coast shooting was halted while I got a crash course from a drama coach on proper oral delivery and tactics to generate an "illusion of enthusiasm" to the camera. But it still didn't quite work, and nobody could figure out why. We continued to shoot around me, and I could sense that I was about to be replaced by one of the runner-ups in the original WGBH competition (who also had written a textbook, had a reputation as being a good teacher, and was still actively engaged in research).

By chance, the next day we were shooting a scene in the program titled "The Self," in which I was discussing and demonstrating verbal and nonverbal differences between high- and low-status communicators. My colleague Patricia Ryan of the drama department at Stanford University, with whom I had taught practicum courses in Psychology and Drama, used a simple theater game to illustrate status transactions, which she argued is at the core of all drama. One of us plays high status, the other low status, and then we reverse roles in the setting of a person waiting and the other arriving, with the minimal text: "Hi," "Hi," "Been waiting long?" "Ages." The low-status person speaks hesitantly; does not make eye contact; has flexible, jerky, bodily movements that taken together convey the impression of being uncoordinated and tentative. By contrast, the high-status person speaks assertively in clear, full sentences, without any hesitation; makes eye contact; moves every part of the body in "unitized" fashion, so that hand, wrist, and arm move as a solid unit when pointing, and head, neck, and shoulders similarly move as if they are rigidly knotted when turning one's head to focus on another person or object. These are some of the body language signals to which people respond nonconsciously in the status communicated by performers such as John Wayne, John F. Kennedy, Ted Koppel, and others in their high-status league.

In the midst of going through this exercise on camera, the eureka flash struck. I had always been somewhat of a low-status teacher/lecturer who was now being forced to play the role of the high-status communicator in the unique frame of the TV personality. I was unaware that I had adopted that low-status teaching style probably so that students would not perceive me as intimidating but as approachable, likable, and one of them. (After all, I was born and raised in a low-income "ghetto" in South Bronx, New York, where the message was to never act uppity and to remember your lowly roots. The stigma to avoid was to have others believe you were someone with an inflated ego, or in the Bronx vernacular, "He thinks who he is.") Status and respect would come from the quality of *what* I said, not *how* I said it. So I would move vigorously about the teaching stage, hands flying, arms waving, gesturing broadly in best Italian fashion, talking fast, sometimes furiously, sometimes not completing sentences except with a finger flourish marking end points. I had done so for innumerable under-graduate classes, for professional psychology audiences, for lectures to civic groups, and even for rich alumni and potential big donors to their alma mater. Across these diverse audiences somehow I had managed to convey my enthusiasm for psychology (the generic genuine brand, not the new illusory TV variety), regardless of status considerations.

I also reduce the distance between teacher and student by directly interacting with my audience even in large lecture halls, asking and answering questions, sharing audiovisual (AV) materials, which we explore together, making jokes, telling personal stories, and singling out individual members of the audience for dialogues or to participate in a demonstration. At times, I have been found to be teetering pre-cariously on the edge of the teaching stage with a deep orchestra pit menacingly close below as I literally try to bridge that gap between teacher and student. Doing all of these things is what conveys my con-cern for making a direct connection with the audience, for getting them as excited with and enamored by psychology as I am—and as my introductory psychology teacher should have been back in 1950.

Well, the TV folks had frozen me in one position, had a crew mem-ber continually signal me when one hand was about to shoot up into the head shot frame, the other hand by then had been safely ensconced into a locked pocket position for the duration of the shoot-ing. They had slowed down my speech, gotten me to speak in unin-terrupted sentences and make direct, unswerving eye contact—with the camera lens. But what came across was a rather frozen fish, a bac-cala, Italian codfish, and not the zesty Sicilian main dish that I was used to serving.

It was only by explicitly acknowledging what I normally do as a low-status teacher, and what those mean people wanted me to do instead as a high-status TV communicator, that I could create an effec-tive, "mindfully" orchestrated compromise. I then started to speak not to the camera lens but to my human audience, a staff person who I positioned next to the camera lens. I made the necessary unitized ges-tures gracefully, but did so now with a sense of humor, imagining that I was a cross between Peter Jennings and Marlon Brando (as the Godfather). I also visualized speaking to a student from a foreign coun-try, so naturally I would slow down my speech, focus on clearer artic-ulation, and speak more forcefully to enable the student to better com-prehend the message. In between takes, I would indulge my low-status self, gesturing maniacally to my newfound friends on the crew to dispel the energy buildup from all that institutionalized limbic suppression. And simple as that, it worked! No need to call in any of the runner-ups, all of whom I now know are naturally high-status teachers and would have made the TV transition more gracefully than

I did but who, in person, were seen as too serious and formidable to the TV staff. So what you see in real life is not what you usually get on TV.

ON THE PATH TO *DISCOVERING PSYCHOLOGY*

We were on our way, but the way was nevertheless slow and circuitous. I wrote about 800 pages of background material, 30 to 50 pages on each of the topic areas featured in one of our 26 programs, in part to educate the TV staff and to provide specific content for the scriptwriter to incorporate. Because all shooting is generally done in sequences arranged for the benefit of the technical crew, there is no continuity in the development of ideas, which was very difficult for me to adjust to because what we do as teachers is build a story, create a compelling scenario. Rather, all shots of me behind a desk were taken at one time for maybe six different programs, then those of me walking to or from a bookcase, followed by scenes from assorted programs of me walking in the woods, down a Stanford arcade, and so forth.

We had to arrange for the 70 or so interviews with leading psychologists, like B. F. Skinner, Neal Miller, David Hubel, and Eleanor Maccoby, as well as with a number of hot newcomers, in their offices or laboratories throughout the country. However, to save money, I was not allowed to travel to the interviewees; instead, I sent my questions plus the required answers the director had to get out of them so as to fit our programmatic needs (some researchers wanted to talk about their new research, which ill-fitted the theme of a given program, and not the old stuff for which they had won a Nobel Prize, for example). Production lasted nearly 3 years and cost about $2.5 million. I now understand that this was cheap for such an ambitious series; cost cutting at every turn helped, as did the nonprofit nature of the venture, with none of us making any profit nor receiving any royalties or residuals from this venture. To get American Psychological Association (APA) approval, I had to relinquish the association of the series with my textbook, which I did willingly to support its generic value for use with any good introductory psychology textbook.

But has it worked? Was it worth it? I think that all psychologists can be proud of the remarkable success of our *Discovering Psychology* series. For me, the series has become a special form of "outreach" teaching that ideally conveys to the general public and to student viewers three things: (a) the scientific foundation of psychological knowledge; (b) the utility and value of that knowledge for a better understanding of and even effective intervention into many societal and individual problems; and (c) the excitement of the intellectual curiosity stimulated by an inquiry into our subject matter, the nature of human nature. Together, these attributes make psychology for me the most wonderfully rich of all disciplines to study and to teach.

And now for the envelope announcing our success in effectively "giving psychology away to the public" through *Discovering Psychology*:

- The series has been shown repeatedly on public television stations throughout the nation over the past 5 years; licensed for broadcast to 7 cable stations and to 8 others through the Mind Extension University, as well as to 36 multiple systems operators and instructional television fixed services (e.g., Intermedia, Viacom, Warner Cable Communications).
- It has been the basis of an Annenberg/CPB project telecourse shown regularly in more than 700 colleges, with more than 60,000 students having received college credit by watching it, reading a textbook, and passing a standardized final examination. Additional colleges and universities have given psychology course credit to thousands of students through their showing of the Discovering Psychology Telecourse, as distributed by the Mind Extension University.
- More than 3,000 sets of the videocassettes have been distributed to colleges and high schools, and over 10,000 individual program cassettes have been sold through December 1995—making it the 5th most popular series among the 43 that are distributed by Annenberg/CPB.
- Selected programs in the series have been used in conjunction with APA's Traveling Psychology Exhibit to generate discussion and inform the public in the many states where APA has taken these wonderful hands-on exhibits in the past 5 years.
- *Discovering Psychology* is currently being shown on television or in college courses internationally in a dozen countries around the globe, with more expected to be added in the near future.

I have catalogued some of the academic and intellectual successes of this special form of outreach teaching, not to promote this specific series, but rather to use it to encourage all those who are dedicated to improving the teaching of psychology to think more broadly about the nature of how we teach. As we move into the new electronic generation of the next millennium, traditional textbooks may give way to interactive CD-ROM disks that supplement the presentation of text with on-line visual and auditory presentations of personally conducted demonstrations of psychological phenomena, important experiments, and statements by many of the psychologists cited. We should all be involved in the planning of such new teaching technologies so as to maximize their effectiveness. However, this may necessitate changing some of what and how we teach in the classroom in order to meet this "insider competition." Similarly, new forms of teaching will surely emerge as teachers and students are linked electronically via the World Wide Web. The physical confines of one's classroom are no longer a constraint on the resources available to any teacher; the world of knowledge is literally at our fingertips and those of our new generation of students.

Philosophy for Teaching the Introductory Psychology Course

I begin my discussion of *why* I teach *how* I teach with personal motivations that I expand using a general theory about what is important to transmit in a lecture-based introduction to psychology class, guided by some course goals and objectives and achieved by a series of general strategies and specific tactics. Let's consider each in turn.

PERSONAL MOTIVATIONS

I want to make a significant difference in the lives of as many of my students as possible; to be liked, admired, and respected by those I teach; and to be remembered as someone who gave fully of himself to the process of teaching, who took intellectual risks, and who always worked to make learning enjoyable as well as a constant intellectual challenge.

TEACHING GOALS

The primary goal is to make my introductory course truly memorable in each student's academic experience by creating a unique learning atmosphere infused with the energy of charismatic teaching. The daily attendance goal is set high at 100%. Students should look forward with eager anticipation to each lecture, as I do, and expect to learn something new and valuable from it, as I do.

TEACHING OBJECTIVES

As paraphrased from my course syllabus, course objectives include the following: to master a broad amount of information (concepts, terms, contributors, history, conceptual perspectives, and principles) about scientific and applied psychology; to understand the use of basic aspects of scientific methodology for answering vital questions about psychology and for testing theoretically derived hypotheses; to appreciate the value of psychological knowledge in applications to everyday life; to become a more critical consumer of information, advertising, propaganda, and persuasive appeals; and finally to become more tolerant of individual and group differences while embracing the richness of human diversity.

LEARNING TASKS

In my introductory psychology course a basic task consists of vocabulary development, then of the development of a range of intellectual skills, with emphasis on descriptive and representation skills, as well as critical thinking, inferential thinking, and verification. I assess these skills with formal examinations, term papers, and experimental projects. In some courses, where there is a proctor for each three students in a "personalized system of instruction," we also rely on individual or small group oral examinations (see Zimbardo, 1977a). Changes in students' personal attitudes are not assessed formally but will be evaluated by each student over the course of her or his lifetime (see Donald, 1989).

TEACHING STRATEGIES

After the most general strategies of aspiring to and practicing at teaching charismatically come those of creating a special, inviting learning context. For me, that means combining affective and cognitive learning; being student-centered; violating some student expectations about course processes; making much of the learning dramatic; integrating visual and auditory inputs to learning; blending education with entertainment; using lectures and readings to go beyond the information given in the textbook and to motivate students to think independently, creatively, and critically—while I model an enthusiasm for psychology.

There are many specific ways to operationalize these strategies in a lecture course in introductory psychology. Before getting to the nitty gritty of what I do and how I organize ideas and materials to achieve particular effects, I would like to detour for a moment to consider a broader context in which any specifics might well be set, that of what it takes to be a charismatic teacher.

CHARISMATIC TEACHING

Anyone can be an effective teacher by working at the fundamental principles of lecture organization and delivery, knowing the course materials well, and putting time and thought into practicing its presentation. Effective teachers are not born that way, they learn to become so by being sensitive to the needs of their students and the context of the instruction and investing lots of time and effort into mastering the logistics and content of the course.

But why be content with that level of acceptable performance for one's lifetime career when, by investing more time, focused effort, and a tad of personal risk, one can "go all the way" and become a charismatic teacher? The charismatic teacher, like one's peers in political and social realms, inspires his or her students to extend their horizons, to willingly endorse and practice recommended actions. Such a teacher imbues ordinary concepts with dynamic vitality, transforming ordinary settings, such as classrooms, into theaters of the mind where the student becomes an engrossed actor in an unfolding drama.

What does it take to become one of *them*? From observations of teachers who demonstrate this elusive special quality (and charismatic figures from other domains), one can extract a number of essential components of the charismatic psychology teacher (see Milojkovic & Zimbardo, 1980).

- High energy level: Actions are powered with a dynamic force; an intensity of purpose is communicated through verbal and nonverbal means.
- Total mastery: Each presentation appears to be thought through completely, with special knowledge apparent of the subject matter, transitions carefully selected, examples aptly chosen, and conclusions emerging naturally from a clearly defined story path.
- Joy of understanding: Delight with the complexity and richness of psychology is immediately communicated through self-disclosures that reveal a sophisticated comprehension of the processes involved in any analysis of the whys and hows of mind and behavior.
- Insatiable curiosity: Never satisfied with current explanations, there is a continual seeking of deeper, more complete analyses, integrating what is typically compartmentalized, and always open to new ideas regardless of source, and especially those from the present audience of students.
- Dramatic appreciation: A profound sense of how to make any topic more interesting by imbuing it with some dramatic flair, an eye toward timing, and a keen sensitivity to the audience's needs, moods, and responsiveness all combine to involve every listener totally—affectively as well as cognitively.
- Sincerity: Risking, yet steering beyond the dangers of being perceived as a "show person" by colleagues, the charismatic teacher

communicates a genuine belief in the importance of the message and an abiding commitment to psychology, thereby leading the audience to acknowledge his or her "communicator credibility."

- Affective involvement: Enmeshed in the "flow" experience of the expanded present moment, the lecturer's emotional reactions are readily expressed to all facets of the teaching endeavor and subject matter, along with a desire to involve the members of the audience equally deeply in their own affective relationship to the ideas being transmitted.

- Unity of purpose: The lecturer lays out the path that audience members will follow to realize their shared goal of becoming intellectually and spiritually enriched by this unique learning experience.

There are some other features of the charismatic teacher one might add, such as flawless presentations, assertiveness of point of view, and positive self-image (not parts of my long suit). Whichever specific dimensions of charisma one wishes to add, omit, or modify, the bottom line for me is that charismatic teaching can be learned and is not necessarily an inherited disposition; it is the product of arduous and well-organized cognitive activity impelled by a burning desire to teach superbly and to make a lasting impression on one's students. So it means caring about teaching, caring about students, caring about psychology, and caring about one's chosen self-identity as a teacher. It also means learning and practicing teaching techniques by observing master teachers and reading the useful advice described in manuals that outline how to teach effectively (see Axelrod, 1976; Benjamin & Lowman, 1981; Bornstein & Quina, 1988; Eble, 1976; Johnson & McKeachie, 1978; Zimbardo & Smith, 1994). However, teaching technique and the scaffolding of a lecture must never overwhelm its intellectual fiber, nor overshadow the central core concepts being communicated. Ideally, they blend into a perfect stew, tasty and nourishing.

BACK TO TEACHING TACTICS

In this section I outline a number of specific features of my classroom teaching that have worked well for me and for other teachers that I have helped train in teaching workshops or graduate teaching assistant practicums.

Tell Stories

I believe that the human mind is exquisitely designed to extract information and remember information that is presented in a story format, with human characters involved in plots or themes. Journalists surely know the validity of this principle as is evidenced by their news articles that begin with an account of a particular person facing a specific problem or challenge, then go on to generalize it to a broader population, and end by bringing the reader back to the solution or continuing dilemma faced by that first person, Johnny or Janie Every Person. Curiously, few psychologists apply this to their teaching: Present information in a story format, as often as possible. Tell a good story, personalize it with real characters, fictitious characters, student characters, or yourself. When possible, use humanizing examples to illustrate abstract points and start from the audience's current experiences and move them to new or different interpretations and appreciations.

Teach People as Well as Principles

Put people at the center of your psychology. For example, in describing a research study, occasionally present it from the phenomenal perspective of a typical participant going through the procedure, rather than always from the abstract characterization of the investigator's experimental and control treatments. I do so by showing slides of my research that always include shots of each key stage in the procedure as faced by one or more research participant, when possible, or telling it as if I were that person entering that research setting. I also have a teaching assistant take photos of me while lecturing from various locations in the lecture hall, so that later on, during the perception lecture, I can show the class the visual reality of their different perspectives within this common setting.

Create a Unique Learning Environment

If you want your students to long remember your course, your psychology, and you, it is essential to package the instructional message in a memorable context. It helps if the context is unique in some ways that differentiate it from all the others in students' experience, so that it violates their expectations about what a traditional lecture class is or ought to be. They should feel comfortable in that setting, feel somehow individuated even in a large lecture hall, yet always feel the presence of an element of the unexpected that might pose a challenge and so keeps them alert.

Students enter my class with background music playing over the speaker system. Sometimes the lyrics reflect the lecture theme (e.g., memory, emotion, or madness), other times the music is energizing or mellow and relaxing, but it is always varied. The use of entry music has four virtues: It rewards those who get to class early by not having to sit in a silent lecture hall waiting for the action to begin; it creates a good feeling in students because it is a special, atypical academic experience while the music soothes their savage intellects; it gets me to class on time by forcing me to be there 10 minutes earlier than I used to in order to start the tape or CD; and finally, the abrupt termination of the music is the discriminative start cue—the lecture starts the moment the music ends.

One lecture per week begins with an open mike period of about 5 minutes wherein there is a microphone available to any student who wants to voice a personal opinion, add a relevant anecdote, challenge a point in a lecture, or complain about course logistics—for the whole class to acknowledge. It may take a few sessions for students to discover that they have really been bestowed this special opportunity to have a public voice. If no one has anything to say, I wait out the allocated time before starting your lecture, so that next time they know that the open mike period is really theirs. My students have reacted very positively to this innovation because it conveys a respect for their input to the course.

Provide a clear, uncluttered conceptual clothesline on which you will hang the key points of the lecture in an overhead transparency outline (prepared with large word-processed fonts, 24- or 30-point size, to be easily seen from the rear of the auditorium). It is there for students to read and copy as they enter class, and for you to return to from time to time in the course of the lecture, so you all know what is generally coming next and where you've already traveled together on that day. Students appreciate having that conceptual organization, especially those that come into class after the opening presentation.

Vary the opening presentation so that sometimes you ask a provocative question, share a personal anecdote, read a newspaper feature that relates to your theme (it is a good idea also to make an enlarged overhead copy to supplement your verbal description), offer an intriguing quote, or use a short video segment as a "lecture launcher." The *Discovering Psychology* series can be cannibalized into a series of brief modules of several minutes' length each that you retape and use to start a lecture. Similarly effective, and even better for some objectives, is to start out with 1 of the 16 modules from the *Candid Camera Classics in Introductory Psychology* that I prepared with their creator, Allen Funt, which is distributed by McGraw-Hill publishers. A *Viewer's Guide/Instructor's Manual* (Zimbardo & Funt, 1993) lays out the themes of each scenario and offers a synopsis, typescript of any dialogue, and Funt's recollections, along with specific advice about how to use them to enhance teaching effectiveness.

Demonstrate Ideas, Concepts, and Experiments

"Don't talk, show me" is the refrain of the heroine in the musical *My Fair Lady*, and it is a principle by which my lectures live. A good demonstration takes a lot of time, effort, and thoughtful planning, but is worth it when it works because it adds to the memorability of the presentation. To be sure, you can often make the same point in less time by just reciting it—but this is what many teachers do most of the time—and most of the students forget it after their "memory dump" postfinals.

One key to creating a good demonstration is always to visualize it from the audience's perspective and not just your own. Another is to make explicit the key conceptual points, or generalizations, you want the audience to take away from this specific instance, doing so either before or afterward, depending on the nature of the demonstration. Keep notes on what worked and what didn't work so that you can move toward perfecting it over repeated presentations in subsequent terms. Also it is important to plan for failure, so have backup material ready in case the demonstration does not work as planned. Another way to reframe this risk of failure is that it poses a challenge to the teacher—as psychologist—to figure out on the spot why a particular demonstration did not work at this presentation. That element of risk makes your teaching more exciting for you.

Below I outline a handful of demonstrations that I have developed to highlight various lecture themes in my course so that I can provide specific guidance on some of the thinking that goes into making demonstrations work. First let's consider some animal demonstrations before turning to human ones with student participants.

Animal Behavior Demonstrations

In earlier teaching days, when I was closer to my Yale behaviorism roots, I created three animal demonstrations. To illustrate the process of Skinnerian shaping of behavior, I created "Hercules, the Amazing Rat." Students observed a (hungry) white rat in a large, clear, plastic, circular enclosure wandering around and then getting food pellets as he approached the protruding bar, and eventually coming to press that bar systematically to deliver those tasty morsels on a regular reinforcement schedule. To make this ordinary demonstration dramatic, the bar was extended outside the chamber so that weights could be attached to it, with large clear markers. The little rat's goal was to keep working ever harder to get his food by exerting more downward force on the bar to counteract the gradually increasing bar weight. At some point, when the metal weights exceed the rat's body weight, he is yanked off the floor as he lets the bar up to eat his just desserts. But our hero quickly learns a new response, that of anchoring his rear claws in the wire mesh provided around the bar. As he pushes down with all his little rat might and the heavy weights lift up, and the food pellet is delivered, "HERCULES!" lights up in a box above the chamber. The recognition of his achievement of this feat of Olympian strength is of course followed by an ovation from his admiring audience.

That same readily viewable enclosure became "Sally's Sex Arena," for a demonstration on the hormonal control of animal sexual behavior. Female rats can be brought into heat at lecture time by injecting them previously with a carefully timed series of hormonal injections. Their behavior in the presence of a male rat is then highly stereotyped into a predictable ritual (see Zimbardo & Barry, 1958). It consists of running away from the male admirer, then stopping suddenly and raising their rump (lordosis). The panting suitor mounts, thrusts, withdraws, and the "run-and-shoot" sexual offense is repeated until the male achieves orgasm. Short time out, and then the carousel ride starts again. Aside from the obvious generic appeal of anything having to do with sex, this demonstration allows the teacher to lay out a series of very precise behavioral predictions about the sexual responses of male and female rats and then of course to have the class consider the differences between sexual scripts that are biologically versus psychologically based.

An animal demonstration of alternative attributions for abnormal behavior—situational or dispositional—was developed around a shuttle-box apparatus that I had built earlier for a study with one of my esteemed Yale mentors, Neal Miller (see Zimbardo & Miller, 1958). The experiment involves two rats that look identical. However, they soon behave very differently. When the first is put into one end of a two-chambered alley (with glass front for viewing), he explores the white side freely, then climbs over the middle barrier and continues exploring the other black chamber before eventually settling down. In stark contrast to Curious Charlie is Terrified Timmy, who races out of the white compartment, leaps over the barrier, and huddles at the far end of the dark chamber. Now let's explore what accounts for this dramatically different set of behaviors taking place in identical environments. Attributions fly freely from the students, almost all focused around the positive traits of the first rat and negative inner qualities of the second. These spurious explanations can be encouraged if the rats are of different colors, white versus hooded, or of different sexes. The actual explanatory difference is the learned fear in the second rat, as he has been conditioned to associate the first white chamber with painful shock to his paws from the electrified grid. The exploratory behavior of the first rat was not extinguished by this aversive conditioning. This situational explanation can be supported by showing a videotape of the prior conditioning procedure. There are some obvious extensions of the traditional message about learned fears to the social domain of "attributional charity." One ought not rush to negative dispositional attributions for behavior that does not make sense or that seems strange—until one has first exhausted all reasonable situational explanations of modifiable behavior.

Human Behavior Demonstrations

Among the many demonstrations I use in the human realm are five that I recommend and briefly discuss here. To enhance what is often perceived by students as a tedious lecture on methodology, I conduct two demonstrations, one of variables that can bias reaction time (RT) and another on the alleged power of extrasensory perception (ESP).

In the first, I start with a bold assertion that my class and I will test with scientific objectivity: "Men are faster than woman." After operationally defining *faster* as more rapid RT in response to an overt stimulus, I then arrange conditions to guarantee the outcome. Female student participants in the rear of the auditorium are arbitrarily called on to shout out their response to a stimulus, thus must yell, "shit," to the firing of a starter's pistol. Their RT is assessed crudely by my wrist watch, in seconds. Male student volunteers are invited up to the stage to respond to a discrete light cue by pressing a button, which is measured by an electronically triggered stopwatch in milliseconds. As student complaints eliminate each of these obvious sources of experimental bias, others are introduced, such as preparatory cuing of the male students while distracting the female students, now both arrayed in front of the same RT apparatus, as well as variations in timing of the stimulus presentations, and so forth. In a short while, psychology neophytes are designing a perfectly controlled experiment to test this controversial hypothesis and realizing the dangers of uncritically accepting conclusions about what "research shows" that they are told repeatedly by the media.

To demonstrate the need to utilize experimental controls at the right place in an experimental design, I involve the class in an ESP trick demonstration. After claiming that I am being trained in ESP so soon will be able to read the minds of students who are "senders," I apologize for now only being able to know precisely what they are thinking by first asking a few questions. The ESP assertion is that I will be able to detect the name and address of anyone in the city phone book that a student selects and mentally sends to me. Three students are asked to assist by having their names arbitrarily drawn from a set of class cards. The first is instructed to "pick any number you think of," and then pass it to the second, who will "scramble it up," and then pass it along to the third who will find that page number in the city phone book and select a target name to be mentally "sent" to me. The class offers a variety of controls, such as blindfolding me, having the three students do their activities outside the lecture hall, or selecting three other participants of their own choosing. I go along with whatever they say, as none of it will make a difference. The central issue is the actual instruction given to the assistants, not my general paraphrase of them.

The first student's written instruction is to pick any three-digit number, in which the first is larger than the last (e.g., 301); the second's "scrambling" is really to reverse the number and subtract the smaller from the larger (301 − 103 = 198); while the third student is instructed to look up that page number (198) and find the specific name that appears at the countdown from the last digit in the end column of the page (eighth name in this example). The student is then supposed to visualize the name and address and use ESP circuits to send it to me. I ask that student several questions, such as whether the individual is male or female, whether there is actually a street address listed, whether there is a full name or initials. Within a maximum of three questions I can select the correct name because a mathematical progression results from the decision rules in my set of instructions (99, 198, 297, 396, 495, etc.).

Before class I memorize the nine names that could possibly be chosen by the students and then decide on what three questions can rule out all but one target person based on the categorical aspects of that set of names. The "show time" part comes after I am sure of that critical name. To add drama and humor I first make slight errors, as in, "I see a huge beast of burden . . . an ox . . . no, you are trying to confuse me, it is a small wily animal, a fox. Could it be Mrs. I. J. Fox?" It works better if the sender writes out the information on an overhead transparency for the class to see so they can participate in the near misses before my inevitable hit with eyes blindfolded.

The methodological point again? There was only one part of the procedure that required strict controls to ensure what I had claimed was indeed being carried out in an operationally valid way—but it never is in all the many times I have conducted this demonstration, nor in magic shows.

Delayed auditory feedback (DAF) is an excellent way to introduce issues of feedback control systems. By using any three-head tape recorder, delays of about a quarter second can be manipulated between talking (into a microphone headset) and hearing (through earphones) what one has said as compared with immediate feedback.

DAF effects are strong: Individuals' speech patterns often break down when they do not get immediate feedback; they talk louder, slower, cycle phrases, stutter, and in some cases are unable to speak if hearing is not immediate. The effects are more pronounced on tasks requiring greater speech coordination, such as singing rather than reading text, and on thoughtful, new material rather than the familiar, such as describing an ideal vacation or a mate. A demonstration would first screen a few volunteers who come to class early, to eliminate those who show weak effects (like choral singers and musicians used to hearing delayed feedback). Then you start with normal feedback on reading a passage from the course text, switch to delay, then description tasks, without and then with delay, and finally have the student participant lead the class in singing, "Row, row, row your boat" first line normal and the rest under DAF conditions. The control of speaking and even of thinking by auditory feedback becomes demonstrably clear—and funny.

Sometimes a simple adjustment makes a tried-and-true demonstration much more effective. I did this with a traditional demonstration of rumor transmission and social memory and in a demonstration of the effects of displaced visual perception.

A powerful demonstration of social aspects of memory utilizes the subway scene image (on an overhead) from Allport and Postman's (1947) study of rumor transmission along with the serial-transmission procedure from Bartlett's (1932) classic research on social memory. The first of five recruited students hears a description of a scene (where there is an apparent racial confrontation) in which I mix central and peripheral details so as to increase the likelihood of distortion. Each successive student comes up to the stage from a hall waiting area, is told what the previous one remembers, and passes the message on. There are always leveling, sharpening, and assimilation processes evident, and sometimes the dramatic transposing of the knife from the White person's hand to that of the Black passenger, or the conflict is totally cooled off as the knife and racial argument are dropped entirely. This demonstration proves more effective when the original scene is projected continuously on the screen behind the participants during each of the story exchanges, so that everyone can monitor the distortions from the original to the current version. It also helps to have a comparison participant who hears the original story along with the first participant, but then does some filler task outside the classroom until invited to recall the story after the final participant. This contrasts minimal and maximal social influences on memory.

How would you cope with a world that was "off target?" What changes would you have to make if suddenly everything you saw was, say, 20° further to the left than its true orientation? This is an introduction to the classic demonstration of displacing (also of invert-ing) the visual field by means of specially designed goggles fitted with prismatic lenses that can be adjusted to change the visual angle of incoming stimulation. We know that humans can make this adjust-ment much faster than animals, but how fast, and what is involved? Usually when I performed this demonstration in a large lecture hall, I would ask a student volunteer to perform a task with the goggles on but set at normal orientation, then the same task through the dis-placed lens, and finally the readjustment when the viewing field was normalized again. Originally, the task was to pick up an object on a table, and sure enough, the student would reach about 20° to the wrong side at first but then gradually make the correct grasp in three to five trials. However, the demonstration was not vivid, especially for those in the back of the room. Redone to enhance its dramatic impact, the demonstration now begins by selecting a student athlete from the audience (e.g., Jim Plunkett, then quarterback on Stanford's varsity football team that would soon win the Rose Bowl). He or she is asked to throw a football to a moving target, a teaching assistant, or you. The student does this accurately under normal viewing con-ditions but is way off target the first few trials with the displaced lenses, throwing the football into the wall rather than at the receiver. Soon, however, the student adjusts perfectly, typically to class applause. Now the surprising part of the demonstration: The student is asked to take the goggles off and make one more accurate throw now that conditions are again "normal"—and the football hero throws the ball way out into the audience—exactly 20° more to the left than the target! The focus of student applause suddenly switches. Analysis of the principles underlying this effect leads to an interest-ing discussion. The basic features of this demonstration are graphi-cally illustrated on the football field in the *Discovering Psychology* pro-gram on sensation and perception.

Demonstrations With Audiovisual Materials

I end this section with mention of two AV-based demonstrations, one that launches my opening lecture and another that comes near the end of the term, each of which serves different course objectives.

The latter is a synchronized slide–tape show on Vincent Van Gogh, in which beautiful color slides of his masterpieces are juxtaposed with his self-portraits that vividly depict his personal deterioration over time. The accompanying music is Don McLean's "Vincent," usually remembered as "starry, starry night," the song's refrain. Appropriate slides flash on, fade in, or fade over other scenes, as dictated by the lyrics of the sad love song (and created using a tape-recorder synchronizer). Most students find it a very emotional experience when the demonstration is set in the context of madness and creativity, supplemented by some background about this fascinating artist's struggles with social convention, personal turmoil, and madness. The idea for this show came from a film made by a master in the development of AV class materials, James Maas, teacher extraordinaire at Cornell University. Although it took me 38 hours to make this 3.5-minute demonstration (including locating and taking all of the photos and learning how to use the synchronized tape-recorder), I can now use it repeatedly in future classes with no further effort and with guaranteed emotional payoffs.

I know of no better way to begin an introductory psychology lecture course then by violating student expectations about the first day of class, their passive roles, and their views about the nature of psychology—than with a demonstration of *violation of expectations*. A full description of the procedure I use is given in my *Candid Camera Instructor's Manual* (Zimbardo & Funt, 1993, pp. 33–40), so I highlight here only the key aspects of this winning demonstration. Shortly after beginning the class by defining psychology and perhaps asking a handful of students what they hope to get from such study, I tell them that instead of talking about psychology, we will do what psychologists actually get paid to do, that is, observe behavior and then try to analyze its causes, effects, and meaning. The 6-minute Candid Camera video "Handsome Teacher" shows four separate pairs of junior high school girls being invited to join the special class of a new, young, handsome teacher. We then observe the differences in their public reactions in his presence and private ones when he is called away. When alone, they laugh, hug, groom themselves, and squeal with apparent delight, as most of my entire class does too.

Question 1, "Why are the girls laughing?," is projected overhead as soon as the video stops, and I entertain and write out student answers to this question about their inferences from their observations. We then move to consider the next overhead question, why they, the students in my class, laughed. This raises issues of introspection. After discussing whether boys would react differently in a comparable situation, the 4-minute Candid Camera video of a provocative "Pretty Teacher" is shown, with even more dramatic results. We then discuss their observations of differences between the two gender groups and finally raise the last question of why I started the course in this way.

One reasonable interpretation of the surprise and humorous reaction of the Candid Camera subjects is that the new teacher violated their *expectations* about what typical teachers look like and how they behave toward students. If someone does not spontaneously generate this explanation, then I do so—for both why the laughter and why I started my course this way. We consider what an expectation is—an anticipation or prediction of some future event based on prior similar circumstances, the psychological processes involved in their formation, and their role in humor, in horror, and as the core aspect of schema.

But what if the teacher violated expectations by being severely handicapped, or what if there was only one student and not a dyad, would laughter still be the common response? What if there was no laugh track? Such "what if?" questions take us into the realm of experimental psychology wherein we manipulate or modify some feature of the setting or process we are studying to determine whether it makes a difference.

Finally, to illustrate the way in which expectations and their violations are studied by psychologists from very different domains, I present a set of brief video clips from *Discovering Psychology:* psychophysiological assessment of surprise at cortical levels by using the P-300 EEG wave form (Emanuel Donchin in Program 1), facial surprise reactions of very young children when observing an impossible event that violates their sense of object permanence (Renee Baillargeon in Program 5), and the classic "Pygmalion effect" of teachers' positive expectations on their subsequent student evaluations (Robert Rosenthal in Program 20). In later lectures, this theme keeps resurfacing—in the role of expectations in classical conditioning, cognitive schema, prejudice, and our reactions to deviant behaviors.

These are but a few of the demonstrations that I have developed to make the course more interesting for me to teach and for students to learn and enjoy. I try to develop one new demonstration each time I teach the course, as a personal challenge and to have enough demonstration materials so that I can rotate them from year to year to keep the course from becoming too predictable.

INVITING GUESTS

My course benefits from the judicious use of guests who are expert in areas outside of my own strengths, some in-house colleagues, some from other departments, and usually one or two from the community. A varsity team coach can talk about motivation and coping with failure; a drama teacher can recruit her students for a dramatic reading of madness in literature; a clinician from Student Health or from a local suicide prevention center can outline available services and current issues in treatment. I have also recruited prostitutes, ex-convicts, politicians, super salespeople, former cult members, and others to help diversify and broaden our perspectives. Not only do such guests add to the mix of your course, they also provide learning experiences for you and give you a day off from a lecture preparation. (Although the arrangement time and inevitable lunch or coffee before or after takes as much or more of your time.)

TESTING

All of the good teacher–student vibrations established by some combination of the above strategies and tactics freeze when the specter of examinations moves to center stage. I have tried a variety of testing procedures to offset the evaluation apprehension that even the best students typically experience. The two procedures that have worked best to improve student test performance and lower test anxiety have been a modified personalized system of instruction (PSI) and partner–team testing.

In the first, I developed courses in which tests on each chapter of the text were administered one-on-one by teaching assistants, who were undergraduate proctors, on a self-paced basis determined by the students, within some timely guidelines. Each of 600 students had his or her own proctor (200 in all) who gave the tests I had prepared in their dormitories, whenever the student was ready to take one during a range of posted personalized testing office hours. Proctors immediately scored the tests, discussed the results, and were permitted to change a score if the student knew the material in question but had misinterpreted the question. The proctors also tried to clarify the reasons for any wrong answers and diagnose sources of problems in studying or test taking. An 80% mastery criterion was required to pass, and each parallel form of the test could be taken up to three times before the student had to drop the course (see Zimbardo, 1977a). It has helped most to have students self-monitor their daily and cumulative study time in this self-paced course, especially in the experimental condition in which weekly progress was monitored by teaching assistants (Yates & Zimbardo, 1977).

In partner–team testing, two students take the multiple choice question exam together but submit only one Scantron and essays, and thus are graded identically. Over 5 years of systematic experimentation with this innovation, we have assigned partners randomly, allowed students to choose their own partners, alternated traditional individual testing with this peer testing during the same term, and given students a choice or required them to participate in team testing. The results have been unequivocally strong across any of these variations. Examination scores have been significantly higher (effect sizes around 0.35) when students take tests with a partner, especially if they also study together and read all of the assigned material but each is primarily responsible for half of it. We have replicated this result repeatedly, in advanced courses, with essay questions, and additional data show that this increase in mean test performance comes with a decrease in the range of scores (the bottom drops out), and a strong endorsement by the students for this type of test arrangement because their greater gain is accompanied by less pain on a variety of dimensions (Zimbardo & Butler, 1996).

Synergistically Combining Teaching and Research

As mentioned earlier, an essential survival tactic I developed for teaching so extensively, while still being motivated to do research intensively, was to find ways of using teaching to get research ideas and then recycling successful research projects back into class lectures (see Zimbardo, 1994). This has meant listening carefully to student ideas, going beyond the facts and established principles usually conveyed in our courses by frequently asking the "what if?" question, and then making it an experimental reality and not merely academic rhetoric. Much of the best research that I have done has come directly out of class exercises, challenges posed by curious undergraduates, or questions raised in seminar discussions. In this category, I include research, such as my experimental studies on deindividuation and violence (Zimbardo, 1970), on the psychology of imprisonment (Zimbardo, Haney, Banks, & Jaffe, 1973), on shyness (Zimbardo, 1977b), on time perspective (Gonzalez & Zimbardo, 1985), and on the normal bases of madness (Zimbardo, Andersen, & Kabat, 1981).

Space limitations allow me only cursory elaboration of this point. Let me provide a few instances. In my social psychology class at NYU, students reading William Golding's *Lord of the Flies* wondered whether the disinhibition of aggression by a leading character, Jack Merridew, after he changed his appearance by painting his face, was psychologically valid or only a novelist's gimmick. Together we designed a series of studies that showed that indeed making people feel anonymous reduced inhibitions on their public actions, so that they could more readily make war or love, as the situation dictated. The Stanford Prison Experiment was first a student-initiated class project that generated such strong affect among the participants that I had to determine whether their reaction was a product of something about their dispositions or the power of the situation. My shyness research came out of the next year's class when a student answered my question about what kind of person embodies both the restrictive–coercive mentality of the guard as well as the passive resistance of the prisoner. A shy student offered the answer, "the shy person," which was better than mine, "the neurotic person." Having never thought much about that alien trait, but realizing its importance, I organized an undergraduate shyness seminar that started a 20-year research program on the causes, correlates, and consequences of shyness in adults and children (Zimbardo, 1986; Zimbardo & Radl, 1981). I use the results and implications of these research projects to energize subsequent class lectures, or to organize entire new courses around them as the ultimate recycling of research back into teaching.

In the Beginning There Was Psychology and Life

I end this chapter by asserting that there is an affinity between good psychology textbooks and good psychology teaching. The introductory psychology course is a holistic enterprise in which all elements combine to influence its memorability for your students. When saddled with a boring textbook, the details of which form the basis of the typically dreary multiple-choice examinations on which their grade is based, students become disenchanted with psychology as a worthwhile domain of knowledge, downgrade the course, and readily execute a memory dump of its contents at the course's end.

Recall from the opening of this chapter my personal story with bad text, bad course, bad taste for all of psychology, and it is as true today. However, we teachers of psychology are fortunate to now have a host of top-quality texts written in styles that engage students' interest and are supplemented by ever-more appealing graphics and colorful art programs. In addition to having a wide choice of available good texts, publishers and psychologist–authors also provide us with valuable instructor's manuals and a host of useful AV materials to support our teaching endeavors. Nevertheless, it is important for psychology teachers to provide constructively critical feedback directly to those authors and publishers about what works, doesn't work, or might work better for you and your students—rather than to keep it to yourself—if these teaching resources are to continue to improve in pedagogically valuable ways. I also believe that the nature and structure of introductory psychology textbooks exert a diffuse impact on the nature and structure of how and what we teach in our general psychology courses.

One approach of most current texts, and many introductory psychology courses, presents each subfield of psychology as a relatively independent domain secluded in its own chapter, without an integrating overall theoretical framework, but rather an eclectic conceptual orientation. Such texts also present psychology as a scientific, research-based approach to understanding the fundamentals of mental and behavioral processes. Increasingly, there is a tendency to make explicit and broaden the links to real-world issues, and those of personal concern to students, that can be classified as "relevant." The texts are mostly "student-centered," not faculty or colleague-centered. They are written typically in engaging styles, with well-orchestrated accompanying graphics and artwork, that make them appealing reading for most students. For teachers who "teach the text," that model dictates the organization and structure of their course as well. As a historical note, I should mention that most of these features were first introduced back in 1937 in the textbook that helped to reshape the teaching of introductory psychology and to enhance its attractiveness to students, Floyd Ruch's *Psychology and Life* (see Gobble, 1988). Its success in that and subsequent editions (now in its 14th; Zimbardo & Gerrig, 1996) have made it the oldest, continuously selling textbook in all fields of psychology.

But what would a new, bold text and innovative introductory course that departed from the traditional model look like? First, it would break down some of the arbitrary, APA-approved specialization boundaries between areas and chapters by attempting greater integration across common ideas, processes, and generalizations. For example, learning and memory need to be meshed, not segregated, as do social development and social psychology. Then it would have greater continuity across chapters with foundations created in earlier chapters being developed and systematically built on in later chapters, rather than each standing alone. It would tell a story, or a set of coherent stories, about aspects of human nature. It would eliminate the excessive reliance on references to colleagues' names to substantiate every statement (giving key ones at the end of chapters, or full details in the manual for instructors and teaching assistants who are usually the only ones who may want to check them out). It would make explicitly clear the most important principles in each area of psychology that students should learn and remember for a lifetime and develop those as chapter themes. And it would not "teach down" to the lowest conceivable student reading level just to be easy, but would be written in such an interesting style that any student would be willing to invest the extra mental effort to "get it" at the level most appropriate to present psychology in the full richness of its depth and breadth.

It is a tall and tough order for text writers, teachers, and publishers to move away from the traditional organization and structure of current introductory psychology to try on this or other new formats. However, as our field changes and student interests change, we will need such innovative texts and courses to best tell our meaningful and memorable story of psychology.

For me, becoming the author of *Psychology and Life* (from the 8th edition on; Ruch & Zimbardo, 1971) has had a salutary effect on my teaching because it forced me to do two new things: gain knowledge across a wider range of areas than I had been using in my prior teaching and develop new course materials after each new edition in order to go beyond what my students were then currently reading. Much of my professional life has been organized around preparing a variety of materials for the introductory psychology course, for its students, and especially for its teachers, in the following ways: writing or coauthoring seven editions and three brief editions of *Psychology and Life*, coediting three readers for this course, cowriting student study guides and workbooks for these editions, developing what has become the model for "full-service" instructor's manuals, and also coauthoring two different texts for the mid-level market of introductory courses (see Dempsey & Zimbardo, 1978; Hammond & Zimbardo, 1988; Zimbardo & Maslach, 1977; Zimbardo & Smith, 1994; Zimbardo & Weber, 1994, 1997).

Perverse production or proper passion? Those readers with a psychoanalytic orientation may readily diagnose these intense efforts as merely an overreaction to my early life achievement failures, as a functional, if somewhat excessive, operating style to undo my one little C grade. I prefer to believe that my passion for psychology has emerged not from a reaction to that historic anomaly, but instead from actively facing up to the continual challenges psychology poses to teachers, researchers, and writers of psychology to better understand, and to more engagingly communicate to our students and the general public, the wonders of the nature of human nature.

References

Allport, G., & Postman, L. J. (1947). *The psychology of rumor*. New York: Holt, Rinehart & Winston.

Axelrod, J. (1976). *The university teacher as artist*. San Francisco: Jossey-Bass.

Bartlett, F. C. (1932). *Remembering: A study of experimental and social psychology*. Cambridge, England: Cambridge University Press.

Benjamin, L. T., Jr., & Lowman, K. D. (Eds.). (1981). *Activities handbook for the teaching of psychology* (Vol. 1). Washington, DC: American Psychological Association.

Bornstein, P., & Quina, K. (Eds.). (1988). *Teaching a psychology of people: Resources for gender and sociocultural awareness.* Washington, DC: American Psychological Association.

Dempsey, D., & Zimbardo, P. G. (1978). *Psychology and you.* Glenview, IL: Scott, Foresman.

Donald, J. G. (1989). *A study of learning in six selected psychology courses: What is learned in the university? Report from the Centre for University Teaching and Learning.* Montreal, Quebec, Canada: McGill University Centre for University Teaching and Learning.

Eble, K E. (1976). *The craft of teaching.* San Francisco: Jossey-Bass.

Gobble, W. E. (1988). Remembering Floyd Ruch. In E. R. Hilgard (Ed.), *Fifty years of psychology: Essays in honor of Floyd Ruch* (pp. i–iii). Glenview, IL: Scott, Foresman.

Gonzalez, A., & Zimbardo, P. G. (1985, March). Time in perspective: The time sense we learn early affects how we do our jobs and enjoy our pleasures. *Psychology Today,* pp. 21–26.

Hammond, A. L., & Zimbardo, P. G. (Eds.). (1988). *Readings in human nature: The best of Science'80–'86.* Glenview, IL: Scott, Foresman.

Johnson, M., & McKeachie, W. J. (1978). *Teaching tips: A guide book for the beginning college teacher* (7th ed.). Lexington, MA: Heath.

Milojkovic, J. D., & Zimbardo, P. G. (1980). Charismatic teaching: Its nature and development. *Proceedings of the Sixth International Conference on Improving Undergraduate Teaching* (pp. 1–8). Lausanne, Switzerland.

Ruch, F. L. (1937). *Psychology and life* (1st–7th eds.). Glenview, IL: Scott, Foresman.

Ruch, F. L., & Zimbardo, P. G. (1971). *Psychology and life* (8th ed.). Glenview, IL: Scott, Foresman.

Yates, B., & Zimbardo, P. G. (1977). Self-monitoring, academic performance and retention of content in a self-paced course. *Journal of Personalized Instruction, 2,* 76–69.

Zimbardo, P. G. (1970). The human choice: Individuation, reason, and order versus deindividuation, impulse, and chaos. In W. J. Arnold & D. Levine (Eds.), *Nebraska Symposium on Motivation* (pp. 237–307). Lincoln: University of Nebraska Press.

Zimbardo, P. G. (1977a). Modified version of personalized system of instruction successfully applied in introductory course for 600 undergraduates and 200 dorm-based proctors. *PSI Newsletter, 5,* pp. 1, 3.

Zimbardo, P. G. (1977b). *Shyness: What it is, what to do about it.* Reading, MA: Addison-Wesley.

Zimbardo, P. G. (1979–1988). *Psychology and life* (10th–12th eds.). Glenview, IL: Scott, Foresman.

Zimbardo, P. G. (1986). The Stanford Shyness Project. In W. H. Jones, J. M. Cheek, & S. R. Briggs (Eds.). *Shyness: Perspectives on research and treatment* (pp. 17–25). New York: Plenum.

Zimbardo, P. G. (1992). *Psychology and life* (13th ed.). New York: Harper Collins.

Zimbardo, P. G. (1994). On the synergy between teaching and research: A personal account of academic "cheating." *Psi Chi, 21,* 13–20.

Zimbardo, P. G., Andersen, S. M., & Kabat, L. G. (1981, June). Induced hearing deficit generates experimental paranoia. *Science, 212,* 1529–1531.

Zimbardo, P. G., & Barry, H. (1958, January 10). The effects of caffeine and chlorpromazine on the sexual behavior of male rats. *Science, 127,* 84–85.

Zimbardo, P. G., & Butler, L. (1996). *Cooperative college examinations: More gain, less pain when students share information and grades.* Unpublished manuscript, Stanford University.

Zimbardo, P. G., & Funt, A. (1993). *Viewer's guide/instructor's manual* [to accompany video of *Candid Camera Classics in Introductory Psychology*]. New York: McGraw-Hill.

Zimbardo, P. G., & Gerrig, R. (1996). *Psychology and life* (14th ed.). New York: Harper Collins.

Zimbardo, P. G., Haney, C., Banks, W. C., & Jaffe, D. (1973, April 8). The mind is a formidable jailer: A Pirandellian prison. *The New York Times Magazine,* Section 6, pp. 36, ff.

Zimbardo, P. G., & Maslach, C. M. (1977). *Psychology for our times: Readings* (2nd ed.). Glenview, IL: Scott, Foresman.

Zimbardo, P. G., & Miller, N. E. (1958). The facilitation of exploration by hunger in rats. *Journal of Comparative and Physiological Psychology, 51,* 43–46.

Zimbardo, P. G., & Radl, S. L. (1981). *The shy child.* New York: McGraw-Hill.

Zimbardo, P. G., & Ruch, F. L. (1975). *Psychology and life (9th ed.).* Glenview, IL: Scott, Foresman.

Zimbardo, P. G., & Smith, G. S. (1994). *Instructor's manual* [to accompany Zimbardo/Weber *Psychology*]. New York: Harper Collins.

Zimbardo, P. G., & Weber, A. L. (1994). *Psychology.* New York: Harper Collins.

Zimbardo, P. G., & Weber, A. L. (1997). *Psychology* (2nd ed.). New York: Longman.

Douglas A. Bernstein

Reflections on Teaching Introductory Psychology

2

I was pleased to be asked to describe my views on teaching introductory psychology and to explain why I became the lead author of a textbook on the subject. However, the prospect also worried me because writing a chapter like this is a little like writing your own obituary. You want to tell the story, but you don't want to sound pretentious. So here's my disclaimer.

The following description of how I teach introductory psychology, and why, is offered as information only. I make no claim to special insight about the best way to teach this, or any other, course. My approach to teaching makes sense to me, but I don't expect everyone to agree with it. I have numerous teaching goals, but I do not pretend to have reached them all, and certainly never two semesters in a row.

With this pathetic effort at humility out of the way, let me tell you how I teach—and why I write about—introductory psychology.

My Approach to Teaching

I began teaching in the psychology department at the University of Illinois at Urbana-Champaign in 1968 with almost no experience as a teacher and absolutely no training in how to teach. Formal preparation for my teaching career came during my final year of graduate school and consisted entirely of a note from the head of the department informing me that I had been assigned a section of introductory psychology that fall. Were my students to be bright-eyed, "I'll-believe-whatever-you-tell-me" 18-year-olds? No, I was to take on a section of 50 evening school students, most of whom were old enough to be my parents and came to class after a full day of work in the real world—tired, savvy, serious, questioning, and expecting a real course from a real teacher.

Needless to say, I did not feel up to the task. All I knew about teaching was what I had seen demonstrated by my own teachers from grade school to grad school. Panic took hold as I realized that I could recall more about what my worst teachers had done wrong than about what the best ones had done right. I longed to turn back the clock and, this time, pay attention to how the good teachers had organized their courses and lectures, led discussions, handled questions, and written exams. I also would have asked them for tips on how to be confident and inspiring. My distress grew as I began to examine textbooks, first because I had no clue how to *order* a textbook, let alone choose one, and second because so much of the material I read was unfamiliar. I recall wondering if 50 minutes of hyperventilation could count as a lecture on biopsychology.

The thought of asking someone for help or advice never crossed my mind. I assumed that I was the only graduate student in my department who didn't know how to teach. If I asked too many questions, perhaps I would lose the teaching assistantship that would be my only source of income. So although I had no intention of ever going to medical school, I decided to base my teaching philosophy on the Hippocratic Oath, or at least the part that says "First of all, do no harm." My idea was to teach in a way that would at least not misinform and that might leave my students with a good impression of psychology and psychologists. The plan was to assign the entire textbook, focus as many lectures as possible on the material that I knew best, and, while testing on every chapter, ask questions that focus on "big" concepts rather than arcane details.

Having this plan did nothing to calm me down on the first night of class. I stopped at two service stations on the way to campus, and, believe me, buying gasoline was the last thing on my mind. Still, the course went better than I had expected. I was shaky, to be sure, and I know I made plenty of mistakes, but several features of my desperation-driven approach served me well enough then that I still rely on them almost three decades later.

First, I continue to view college students, regardless of their age, as responsible adults whose task it is to learn textbook material whether I lecture on it or not. Even if it were possible to cover an entire textbook in class, students have a lot of learning to do when their teachers are not around.

Second, I still try to spend as much class time as possible on material that I like and understand. Fortunately, this now includes a wider range of topics than before, so I no longer have to skip over certain processes, such as vision, or certain organs, such as the brain. I want to show students how interesting and important psychology can be, so I usually focus my lectures on the things I think students will find fascinating once they understand them. I punctuate my lectures with lots of demonstrations and classroom activities, and I don't worry very much about what I have to leave out. I have found that this use of class time helps motivate students to read, or even reread, their textbook, to ask questions and make comments in class, and to visit me during my office hours for discussion and clarification. I also find that doing things that stimulate my students in the classroom helps maintain my enthusiasm for teaching. Knowing that I am going to surprise, delight, confound, or challenge my students in tomorrow's class continues to make teaching—and planning my teaching—one of the most exciting and enjoyable aspects of my life.

Third, I still find it best to be myself in class—and not to take myself too seriously. I had little choice in the matter with that first class; many of those students were clearly skeptical about whether I belonged at the front of the classroom. It would have been disastrous had I tried to play the "tough teacher" role by insisting on being called "Mr. Bernstein" or making sarcastic remarks about late-arriving students. But even as my confidence has grown over the years, I still feel most comfortable when I let my students see me as I am, even when it means doing things that some of my own teachers would have frowned on. For example, I recall laughing along with my students one spring day when a pair of dogs charged through our classroom's open door and proceeded to have sex. (I can think of at least one former teacher of mine who would surely have tried to continue with his lecture.) Similarly, I am as quick now as I was as a graduate student to acknowledge when I don't know the answer to a student's question. Knowing that I don't have to appear omniscient makes my classes, and the questions students ask in them, seem more challenging than threatening.

Finally, I still try to test students on material that although not always easy, I consider important enough to be worth knowing when the course is over. And whether essay or multiple choice, my questions almost always test students' ability to *apply*, not just recall, what they have learned. For example, I tend to stay away from questions like "Which of the following substances is *not* a neurotransmitter?" I would much rather ask something like this: "Leshon has been severely depressed lately. According to the biological approach to psychopathology, which of the following neurotransmitters is most likely to be involved in his disorder?" I think it is more important for an introductory student to know the answer to the latter question than the former. Even students who miss such questions can understand why I ask them.

My Course and My Students

Until 1984, the courses I taught at the University of Illinois were all in the clinical area: abnormal, methods of treatment, psychotherapy practicum, research design, and the like. That year, probably because word had leaked out about my one-semester experience with the introductory course 17 years earlier, I was asked to take over as director of our department's Introductory Psychology Program. Psychology 100 enrolls nearly 4,000 students each year, so in addition to teaching my own students, I became responsible for selecting, training, monitoring, and evaluating the graduate student instructors who teach all of the other students.[1] (For better or for worse, I try to encourage in those I supervise the same values, policies, and methods I apply in my own classes.) Section sizes in this one-semester course range from 15 students in the honors seminar to amphitheater crowds of 350 or more. Most sections enroll about 60 students. I usually teach the honors course, but I have also taught sections as large as 750 students.

Evaluation of student performance in Psychology 100 is utterly objective and depends entirely on how many points a student earns out of a possible 300. Students in all sections take the same two multiple choice examinations—an 80-point midterm and a 100-point final. One hundred more points can be earned through some combination of quizzes, short papers, and other work assigned at the discretion of each instructor, and 20 points are awarded for participating in psychology experiments. (The honors section follows the same system, but its exams and quizzes are take-home essays, and a 15-page term paper is required.)

Most Psychology 100 students are in their first year of college, and for many, the introductory course will be their only psychology course. I do not believe that this is my fault. In fact, I bet that because of me,

---

[1]This enormous task would be impossible without the help of Sandra Schweighart Goss, who serves as associate course director.

thousands of students over the years have become psychology majors—and even psychologists. Hundreds, at least. OK, I know of *one* case for sure in which I inspired a student to go to graduate school in psychology. He went on to become a professor at a major university where he conducts important research and has written a competing introductory psychology textbook—proving once again that no good deed ever goes unpunished.

My Goals in Teaching Introductory Psychology

Such bizarre cases aside, my approach to teaching is shaped by the recognition that most students take the introductory psychology course because it (a) sounds more interesting than sociology, (b) satisfies a general education requirement in the behavioral sciences, and (c) is all common sense and intuition. In other words, whether I like it or not, most introductory students are not as immediately interested in all aspects of my course as I wish they were, and certainly not as interested as I am. They are taking several courses in addition to mine, and they are not necessarily eager to read the textbook. Worst of all, and in spite of my best efforts, it is unlikely that most of my students will remember for very long the details of what I have taught and what they have read.

Yet, teaching introductory psychology leaves me neither depressed nor disappointed. Indeed, I suspect that when faculty has a bad experience with this course, the problem can often be traced not so much to student apathy or teacher incompetence, as to unrealistic, even counterproductive, expectations and goals. My goals in Psychology 100 are quite modest, but because they are attainable I think the course works. I try to introduce psychology in a way that students are likely to enjoy, appreciate, and understand. Over the years, I have come to think of myself less as a taskmaster (although my course is a tough one) and more as a museum guide—a person who gives visitors a map of the exhibits, knowing that they will not have time to explore them all in detail but hoping that the experience will either encourage future visits or at least bring good reviews. In short, I try to keep in mind that even if all of my students wanted to hear it, it is impossible to tell the whole story of psychology in one semester. I try to help students learn as much psychology as they have time for and, in the process, show them that the discipline is far more diverse and interesting and important than they might have realized. I think this general goal can be accomplished regardless of whether students remember a lot of specific facts about psychology. My more specific goals for the introductory course follow.

PORTRAY PSYCHOLOGY AS AN EMPIRICAL SCIENCE BASED ON CRITICAL THINKING

I spend about two class sessions at the beginning of the course describing the empirical approach, the methods of scientific research, and how psychologists apply critical thinking processes in studying all aspects of behavior and mental processes. Many students have little interest in these abstract research principles and critical thinking methods, but that's before they find out that I have psychic powers. During the last few minutes of the first class period, I perform a few very simple, but very impressive, magic tricks. I describe these tricks as demonstrations of the psychic ability I allegedly acquired as the result of a closed head injury. When the class is suitably impressed with my "power," I confess to having used trickery. I then challenge the students to spend some time before the next class session applying their critical thinking skills (and the methods described in the assigned chapter on Research Methods) to discover how the tricks were done.[2]

When the class meets again, the students are inevitably motivated to talk about research methods that might help them figure out how I could have fooled them so convincingly. To highlight the need to use these methods in the context of critical thinking, I organize discussion of the psychic tricks around a five-step analytic process. (The steps take the form of five questions: What am I being asked to believe? What evidence is available to support the assertion? Are there alternative ways of interpreting the evidence? What additional evidence would help to evaluate the alternatives? What conclusions are most reasonable?) The discussion tends to focus on the third and fourth steps: alternative explanations for my apparent psychic abilities and the best methods for evaluating those alternatives. I encourage the students to state their alternative explanations as hypotheses and to design—as a group or in small groups—research methods (experiments, usually) for testing their hypotheses. I have found that this session does a reasonably good job of highlighting the general value of research methods and critical thinking for evaluating any phenomenon or claim, from infomercials to political speeches. (In fact, if graduate student instructors tell me they are not comfortable doing a "psychic" act, I suggest that they use other critical thinking targets instead: TV com-

---

[2] I got this idea from Morris (1981).

mercials, magazine ads, and direct mail promotional pieces are ideal.) It also gives me the opportunity to point out that psychologists use the same critical thinking process and the same range of research methods. I note that these methods will be encountered throughout the textbook and the lectures and that the five-step process will be used throughout the course in evaluating the results of all kinds of psychological research.

In my honors section, I follow up on the psychic analysis by assigning small groups of students to read, critically evaluate, and then redesign research articles I have selected for them from psychological journals. The write-ups and class presentations describing the results of their five-step analyses help create in the students the kind of reasonable skepticism about psychological research that I like to see.

PORTRAY PSYCHOLOGICAL KNOWLEDGE AS DYNAMIC, NOT STATIC

I have found that most students want simple, clear, and final answers to questions such as, Is personality inherited? Does TV violence cause aggression? Does therapy work? and Which theory of prejudice is right? They are frustrated when I don't give them what they want, but I try to help them understand why it has to be this way. To help reach this goal, I am forever reminding students that the process of critical thinking and the continuous flow of research arising from it tend to raise questions as well as answer them. I repeatedly emphasize that the question, "What conclusions are most reasonable?" really means "What conclusions are most reasonable given the evidence available so far?" I also highlight many of the questions in our field that simply cannot be answered with a simple yes or no. I point out that this situation does not arise because psychology is "just a matter of opinion" or because psychologists are incompetent, but because the phenomena under study are so complex that the "correct" answers often turn out to be "It depends on the interaction of x, y, and z" or "We don't yet know for sure."

To help convince students that I am not just making this up to save face, I send them out in teams of two to do a simple observation and recording of the walking speed of males and females in a public place.[3] The difficulties they encounter—in obtaining valid measurements, in selecting subjects for observation, in preventing extraneous factors (such as slopes, crowds, or weather) from contaminating results, in guarding against inadvertently cueing each other as to when each starts

---

[3] I got this idea from Stephen Buggie at Presbyterian College, Clinton, South Carolina.

and stops timing, and in a dozen other aspects of the project—go a long way toward helping them appreciate the task researchers face in studying "simple" topics such as interpersonal attraction or hunger. I also remind students that like the psychologists whose work they explore, they must learn to tolerate a certain amount of uncertainty.

In short, my goal is to emphasize the inherent complexity of psychological phenomena and the evolving nature of knowledge about behavior and mental processes. Doing so consistently throughout the semester helps my students accept this aspect of scientific reality, but they still aren't too happy about it.

PORTRAY THE BREADTH AND DIVERSITY OF PSYCHOLOGY

A wise colleague once told me that we are forced to lie to introductory psychology students because we don't have time to tell them the truth. I think this is especially true for those of us who teach the course in one semester. Those who teach a two-semester course have time to tell more of the truth, but even they must leave out a lot of material. (The ideal, eight-semester course poses some practical problems.) So in line with my museum guide analogy, my goal is to at least acquaint students with all of the subfields of psychology even though I am not able to spend much time on any of them.

I know I will never reach this goal if the students do not read the entire textbook, so as noted earlier, I assign every chapter and make all of the material in them fair game for testing, regardless of whether it is covered in class. To help the students read at a steady pace rather than merely cram for the midterm and final, at least five quizzes are administered throughout the semester. Students who keep up with their reading assignments are the ones most likely to notice the breadth of the field. I am always gratified to hear them express surprise when they discover that there is more to psychology than clinical psychology, the area with which they tend to be most familiar. I feel I have done my job if my students go home and tell their parents about subfields such as biological, cognitive, social, and developmental psychology too. In my wildest dreams, a student of mine meets a psychologist on a plane and asks, "What kind of psychologist are you?" instead of "Uh-oh, I bet you're going to analyze me."

PROMOTE ACTIVE LEARNING

As Martha Stewart might say, learning by doing as well as by watching or listening is "a good thing." I do try to encourage active learning, not only in the hope that it will help students think about and remember what happens in class but also because I think these experiences will stimulate them to read the textbook with greater interest and enthusiasm. In my experience, students enjoy the book more (even though reading it is "work") when they are reading about things that have come alive for them in class.

There are many ways of promoting active learning, but my favorite approach is to conduct classroom activities that involve every student in demonstrations of psychological principles, concepts, or research findings. Examples of these activities abound in handbooks (Benjamin, Blair-Broeker, Ernst, & Nodine, in press; Benjamin, Daniel, & Brewer, 1985; Benjamin & Lowman, 1981; Makosky, Selice, Sileo, & Whittemore, 1990; Makosky, Whittemore, & Rogers, 1987; Ware & Johnson, 1996), in the instructor's manuals that accompany introductory psychology textbooks, and in many other sources (including Internet news groups such as Teaching In Psychological Sciences, or TIPS).[4] Just one illustration will suffice here. Rather than merely lecturing on the concept of compliance in the social psychology unit of the course, I begin by asking the class to do a set of utterly pointless things, such as hopping on one foot, giving me a round of applause, or exchanging seats. Inevitably, every student follows these instructions to the letter, and I initiate the discussion of compliance by asking them why they did so. The social bases for compliance are soon being described and debated. Asking the entire class, rather than one student, to do silly things gives this activity special value, because it makes it impossible for anyone to say "I wouldn't have done that." Students who have had this classroom experience usually want to read more about the processes involved.

EMPHASIZE THE IMPORTANCE OF PSYCHOLOGY IN EVERYDAY LIFE

Students tend to appreciate the importance of research methods most when applying them to evaluate psychic power or other claims. Similarly, students tell me that the psychological concepts and principles covered in the introductory course seem to make more sense, and "matter" more, when I describe their importance in everyday life. Fortunately, the diversity of our discipline and the wide range of appli-

---

[4] To subscribe to TIPS, send SUBSCRIBE TIPS YOURFIRSTNAME YOURLASTNAME TO LISTSERV@FRE.FSU.UMD.EDU (INTERNET). Ideas for activities may also be available on World Wide Web home pages maintained by the Society for the Teaching of Psychology (Division 2 of the American Psychological Association) at HTTP://SPSP.CLARION.EDU/DIVISION2/d2.HTML GE.HTM and by Teaching of Psychology in the Secondary Schools, or TOPSS (HTTP://SPSP.CLARION.EDU/topss/TOPSS.HTM top).

cations of psychological research make this easy to do. The trick, I think, is to remember to do it.

I begin my efforts to emphasize the practical importance of psychology early in the course by asking the class to tell me what surprised them about the subfields of psychology described in the opening chapter of the textbook. They usually mention areas such as industrial/organizational psychology, health psychology, engineering psychology, and biological psychology. I then say a few words about each area mentioned and include one or two examples of how research in the area has been applied, such as in personnel selection and conflict resolution, safe-sex and anti-smoking campaigns, automotive and aviation safety, and neuropsychological assessment of brain damage. I also mention some of the career opportunities in each area and remind the students that they will find many more examples as they read the text. Then, I reinforce that message by working into each lecture additional examples of the application of other basic principles of psychology in areas such as law, medicine, architecture, and computer science. I also bring to class each day a newspaper or magazine article illustrating another way in which psychology affects daily life—everything from new psychotherapy methods to insanity pleas to human-factors-influenced product designs. Soon, my students are doing this too.

Emphasizing the practical value of psychological research and practice is important not only because it helps students to learn more about our discipline but also because it may ultimately influence the public and private support psychology receives. Some of our students will become governors, congressional representatives (or staffers), or philanthropists. And even those who do not assume positions from which they can directly benefit psychology, as voters, all of them will have an indirect impact on our discipline. We do not have many opportunities to personally tell a senator why funding for psychological research ought to remain in the National Science Foundation budget, but there is plenty of time in class to give the future legislators a lasting impression of the value of psychological science. When we walk into the classroom, we don't just teach psychology; we also help to shape public opinion about its value to society.

PORTRAY PSYCHOLOGY AS AN INTEGRATED DISCIPLINE

"What does the eye have to do with psychology?" This question, blurted out after class one day, helped me to understand why my students' own eyes began to glaze over during my lectures on neuroanatomy, vision, and hearing. Looking back, I realize that the earliest versions of my introductory course must have struck students as a train wreck of randomly selected topics. A lecture on plant care would probably not have surprised them any more than my lecture on depth perception. For some, I bet, it was only the sight of the words *personality* and *psychopathology* on the syllabus that prevented them from dropping the course. I had simply forgotten to provide a coherent framework that showed how the apparently disparate course topics all fit together. I'm not sure why this happened. Maybe I was just so pleased at now being able to cover topics I had skipped during my first attempt at teaching that it never occurred to me that students would have no clue *why* I was covering them. In any case, I try to solve the "glazed eyes" problem in three ways.

First, when presenting the definition of psychology, I emphasize that the concept of "behavior and mental processes" includes everything from the activity of single cells to the interactions of groups. As a quick active learning illustration, I ask the class to raise their right hands on my count of three. We then discuss the biological and cognitive processes that allowed each person to detect the incoming stimulus; perceive, understand, and remember my instruction; decide what to do; and execute the response. When I ask the students to imagine how they would do at this simple task if they had no sensory or motor neurons, they begin to see why the textbook contains chapters on biological psychology, sensation, and perception.

Second, I cover the material on developmental psychology very early—right after the research methods unit—in order to emphasize that each individual, including each student in the class, represents a wondrous integration of specialized cells and processes that during the rest of the course, we will examine in more detail.

Finally, I try to include in every class session examples of how concepts, principles, and research results from one of psychology's subfields are related to, apply in, and help us understand other subfields. An obvious example is how the explanatory theories and drug treatments for certain psychological disorders are related to the action of certain neurotransmitters on nerve cell activity in certain parts of the brain. I also like to point out that the same kinds of perceptual biases that can influence us to see an ambiguous figure one way or another can also influence our perception of people, sometimes leading to self-fulfilling prophesies and prejudice.

Nothing gives me more pleasure as a teacher than hearing a student say that he or she is beginning to see how "all this stuff fits together." This does not happen every day, but often enough to make my efforts seem worthwhile. Indeed, helping students to see psychology's "big picture" and to appreciate the importance of what psychologists have accomplished so far is a large part of what I try to accomplish as a teacher.

Writing an Introductory Textbook: Don't "Just Do It"

If current trends continue, by the year 2010 every psychology faculty member in North America will have written an introductory psychology textbook. If you are currently thinking of doing so—or if someone is trying to talk you into doing so—I can offer only one piece of advice: Don't do it unless you have at least one reason to write the book that is more important to you than the prospect of making money.

I am speaking from the heart here, because until my coauthors and I began our introductory textbook project, I had no idea how much time and effort it would take. We spent about 5 years writing the first edition, and each new edition consumes us nearly full-time for 18 months. My conversations with numerous other introductory text authors suggest that their experiences are about the same. Is it "worth it?" I think so, but not as a paying job. If your book is successful, it is likely to bring a financial return that—when divided by the number of hours you spend writing it—is about what you would earn at a fast food restaurant. There have to be other reasons to take on the challenge. The prospect of a royalty check 6 years hence is probably not going to be enough to keep you going when the book is behind schedule, many other responsibilities demand attention, and after working for an entire morning on a single page, you still can't get it to read just right.

Why did I do it? The idea of writing an introductory psychology text occurred to me only after being asked by a publisher to review someone else's book proposal. At a dinner meeting with the company's psychology editor a few weeks later, I made the mistake of being a little too specific in describing how I thought the proposal might be improved. Most of my ideas involved tailoring the book to meet the teaching goals I have already described. Without thinking where it might lead, I said that if it were me, I would want to create a book that would reinforce some of the most important messages I try to convey in class: (a) that psychology is an empirical science, (b) that its numerous subfields are related, (c) that one must think critically about psychological research, and (d) that the results of that research are being widely applied in the service of human health, productivity, and welfare. The editor smiled, refilled my wine glass, and asked if I had ever thought of writing a book like that.

The rest, as they say, is history or, in this case, psychology. The features of the book that resulted from that conversation were shaped by the desire to do a better job of teaching introductory psychology, and my coauthors and I keep that in mind as we work on each new edition.

References

Benjamin, L. T., Jr., Blair-Broeker, C., Ernst, R. M., & Nodine, B. F. (Eds.). (in press). *Activities handbook for the teaching of psychology* (Vol. 4). Washington, DC: American Psychological Association.

Benjamin, L. T., Jr., Daniel, R. S., & Brewer, C. L. (Eds.). (1985). *Handbook for teaching introductory psychology*. Hillsdale, NJ: Erlbaum.

Benjamin, L. T., Jr., & Lowman, K. D. (Eds.). (1981). *Activities handbook for the teaching of psychology* (Vol. 1). Washington, DC: American Psychological Association.

Makosky, V. P., Selice, S., Sileo, C. C., & Whittemore, L. G. (Eds.). (1990). *Activities handbook for the teaching of psychology* (Vol. 3). Washington, DC: American Psychological Association.

Makosky, V. P., Whittemore, L. G., & Rogers, A. M. (Eds.). (1987). *Activities handbook for the teaching of psychology* (Vol. 2). Washington, DC: American Psychological Association.

Morris, S. (1981). Believing in ESP: Effects of dehoaxing. In K. Frazier (Ed.), *Paranormal borderlands of science* (pp. 32–45). Buffalo, NY: Prometheus Books.

Ware, M., & Johnson, D. E. (Eds.). (1996). *Handbook of demonstrations and activities in the teaching of psychology* (Vols. 1–3). Hillsdale, NJ: Erlbaum.

Peter Gray

Teaching Is a Scholarly Activity:

The Idea-Centered Approach to Introducing Psychology

3

Perhaps you recall this Doonesbury comic strip episode, from about 10 years ago: A professor is lecturing and begins by making some moderately controversial statements. He notices that none of his students are bothered by his statements; they're just writing them down. So he makes increasingly controversial statements, in an increasingly frenetic manner, until finally he shouts, "Democracy is the source of all evil! Up is down! Right is wrong!" The students continue to write. In the last panel one student leans over to another and says, "Boy, this course is really getting interesting," and the other replies, "Yeah, I didn't know half this stuff."

When that strip first appeared I laughed at it for much the same reason that college professors everywhere did. "Yes, that's how students are these days," I thought. Now I think of it differently, as a comment not so much about students as about teaching. When teaching consists mostly of the presentation of statements to be memorized for tests, students learn that their task is to record and feed back, not to think. "Democracy is evil" is nonsense, but "democracy is good" is also nonsense when presented without thoughtful elaboration. Good for what? Good compared with what? Good for what reasons and according to what evidence? Not much can be done with unelaborated statements except to write them down and memorize them.

Most of us who teach introductory psychology recognize that good teaching is more than the conveyance of factual information. Most of us want to engage students intellectually with ideas in psychology. We want students to think about and question what we teach, not simply memorize our statements and feed them back. However, given an educational system in which students' chief rewards are grades on tests and our chief product is the end-of-term grade list, we too often lose track of the larger purpose and teach in ways that run counter to it.

It is useful to remind ourselves of the intimate link between scholarship and teaching. If scholarship is at all public, it involves teaching. Whenever we write an article, or present a colloquium, or discuss an idea with colleagues at a brown-bag luncheon or casually in the hallway, we are teaching. We are sharing our thoughts in a manner designed to educate and convince others, while at the same time eliciting thoughts and questions that improve our own thinking. Ideally, and sometimes in actual fact, introducing psychology is like all those other forms of teaching. The main difference is that in introducing psychology we are dealing with the most basic ideas of our discipline and with an audience that is naive about them. The naive audience forces us to phrase ideas as clearly as possible, to support them from scratch with logic and evidence, and to show why they are worth thinking about. From this perspective, teaching introductory psychology may be the most intellectually challenging of all our scholarly activities. When we accept that challenge and work at it, some of our students begin to think and argue with us, and we learn from them as they learn from us.

In this chapter I describe an approach to introducing psychology that is designed to make the course a scholarly adventure for students and instructor both. The essence of the approach is to focus explicitly on ideas as the subject matter of the course, rather than on facts, terms, topics, textbook pages, the unsupported opinions of famous psychologists, or any of the other substitutes for ideas that may attempt to force their way to center stage. An idea, by definition, is something to think about; it is something to defend or refute with evidence and logic. I begin with a discussion of the elements of idea-centered teaching and then suggest some specific ways to help students meet the challenges of an idea-centered course (see also Gray, 1993; Prawat, 1991).

Elements of Idea-Centered Teaching

THE IDEA-BASED LECTURE

Imagine, first, a traditional lecture on Freud (a lecture I had given at least a dozen times before I realized its inadequacy). The lecturer summarizes, in 50 minutes, Freud's tripartite division of the mind, his five stages of psychosexual development, a half dozen defense mechanisms, and three tenets of Freud's approach to psychotherapy. It is an easy, comfortable lecture for all concerned. The lecturer can easily rattle off and elaborate on the well-learned definitions; the students can write the definitions down in full knowledge that memorizing them will improve their performance on the next test; and nobody has to risk putting forth original thoughts or arguments. Everyone feels that education has occurred: Information has been transferred.

Now imagine an idea-based lecture inspired by the work of Freud. The lecturer begins: "The idea I want to talk about today (which is written on the board) is this: *The human mind actively defends itself against certain kinds of knowledge as a means of reducing anxiety.* Sigmund Freud developed this idea more than 80 years ago, but even today it is controversial. Was Freud right?" After this introduction, the lecturer elaborates on the idea to make it clear; asks students for their opinions on it and why they hold them; describes Freud's own evidence for the idea, including some of the clinical observations he was trying to explain; offers counterarguments to Freud's; describes some recent research that bears on the question; asks students if they can think of new ways of testing the idea; offers a tentative conclusion that qualifies or delimits the idea; and asks students whether they tend to agree or disagree with the conclusion. In the course of the lecture, a good deal of factual information is imparted, some new terms are introduced and defined, and some points of research methodology are clarified, but the focus throughout is on the idea. Moreover, the idea is not just Freud's. It, or some rendition of it (or perhaps a negation of it) is also the lecturer's idea, and in varying degrees and versions it becomes the students' idea.

In the short run, the idea-based approach has both advantages and disadvantages. Some students see the advantages right off. They are pleased that the lecturer treats them as intellectually mature, values their thoughts, presents the facts and terms in a context that makes them meaningful, and initiates controversy that sometimes continues even after the class ends. Others complain. Even among those who followed and participated in the arguments, some express confusion as to what if anything they have "learned," or they ask, "What are we responsible for?" Idea-based lectures are also, at first, harder for most instructors to prepare than are fact- or definition-based lectures.

In the long run, however, for the purpose of education and for the instructor's own intellectual satisfaction, all advantage goes to the idea-based approach. There is little worth memorizing or reciting in psychology, but there are many ideas and arguments worth thinking about. In idea-centered courses instructors gain ever greater respect for their students' intellects, and students learn to respect their own intellects. Most of us who teach psychology at the college level entered the discipline because we are excited by ideas in psychology. Idea-centered teaching allows us to manifest that excitement and infect others with it.

I am sometimes asked: Do students have to learn the vocabulary of psychology before they can understand and think about the ideas? My answer is no. In fact, the reverse is true. Students must understand and think about the ideas before the technical terms can have real meaning. For example, the term *operant conditioning* has meaning in the light of a certain set of ideas about learning and how to study it, but it can cut thought short in those who have not considered those ideas, because it misleads them into thinking they have learned something important by learning a definition. In an idea-centered course students see their main task not as learning vocabulary but as thinking about ideas. The new words follow easily and are certainly useful for communication, once the ideas are clear and are deemed worth thinking and talking about.

CHOICE AND DEVELOPMENT OF IDEAS

Every realm of psychology, even those that seem most factual, can be characterized as a set of ideas about behavior and the processes that control or influence it. For instance, a central idea in physiological psychology is that the nervous system is divisible into functionally discrete components, which operate in a hierarchical manner to control behavior. A lecture supporting this idea might begin with a discussion of the logic of any hierarchical control mechanism and then move to neuroanatomical and lesion-study evidence that the nervous system indeed operates as a hierarchy. Such a lecture may include many anatomical facts and specific findings concerning the behavioral effects of lesions at different levels in the nervous system, but each fact and finding serves the purpose of testing or elaborating on a single idea.

Here is a sample of other ideas suitable as lecture topics, each from a different realm of psychology: (a) The more deeply we think about an item of information, and the more we link it mentally to other items, the more likely we are to remember it in the future. (That idea not only helps students make sense of many memory phenomena but also illustrates one value of the idea-centered learning that they are experiencing.) (b) The way we think is strongly influenced by the words and structure of our language (the idea of linguistic relativity). (c) Human beings have a remarkably strong desire for approval by other human beings nearby and will behave in seemingly irrational ways to secure it. (An enormous amount of the social influence literature is relevant to this idea.) (d) The symptoms of mental disorders are not qualitatively different from experiences that most of us have had; they differ only in degree.

The best ideas to develop in lectures are those that are central to the field, are neither obviously right nor obviously wrong, are testable with logic and evidence, and are interesting to the lecturer and therefore potentially interesting to students. One idea per lecture is a worthy average to aim for; but sometimes two or three related ideas can be developed adequately in a single lecture, and other times a single idea may span two or three lectures. In my own course, in addition to the separate ideas for individual lectures, I use evolution by natural selection as an integrating theme. Elsewhere I have described how this theme, along with the functionalist perspective it underlies, helps student think about the most fundamental ideas in psychology, provides a foundation for critiquing classic psychological theories, promotes a cross-cultural perspective, helps students overcome their bias to think of pathology before thinking of function, and helps students understand the rationales for cross-species comparisons in psychology (Gray, 1996).

Idea-based lectures need not follow any standard formula, but you may find the following guidelines helpful as a prototype:

- State the idea clearly as the topic of the lecture and have it on the blackboard or a transparency for repeated reference as the lecture progresses. Elaborate on the idea in a manner that makes it interesting and demonstrates its real-life relevance, and say something about its historical origin. Sometimes the idea can be illustrated or exemplified with a demonstration, class experiment, or dramatic story, and in that case the demonstration, experiment, or story may precede and lead logically to the statement of the idea.
- Invite students to share their own initial opinions about the idea and why they hold them. This helps students become intellectually engaged with the idea and helps prove to them that they are capable of thinking like psychologists. Students' comments often anticipate or supplement the lecture's arguments in ways that prove useful as the lecture develops. In a large class opinions may be demonstrated by a show of hands for and against, followed by a sample of arguments on both sides. Students' arguments can be summarized on a transparency as they are stated, which makes it easy to return to them later.
- Devote most of the lecture to evidence and logic that supports, refutes, or delimits the idea. This can be much facilitated by the

use of transparencies or other graphics, prepared in advance, including flow charts of the logic of particular studies and graphs or tables of results.

▪ At the end, invite students to share their critical reactions to the arguments presented in lecture. Sometimes this is best done as a brief writing assignment, in which case some of the most compelling reactions can be read at the beginning of the next lecture. The logical assessment of evidence to test ideas is the essence of psychology (or any other science), and by involving students in that process we involve them in psychology.

THE COMPLEMENTARY FUNCTIONS OF TEXTBOOK AND LECTURES

For an idea-based course, a good textbook and a good set of lectures have much in common. Both should focus attention on ideas and subordinate facts, terms, and names to those ideas. Both should be intellectually engaging to students. Both should challenge students to think critically at their highest level; neither should condescend. In other respects, however, the two differ from one another and serve complementary functions.

Lectures, more than textbooks, permit instructors to define their own course and to bring their own personalities to bear. Lectures permit students to see, in flesh and blood, a person thinking about ideas in psychology. Lecturer A may be excited about humanistic psychology and devote three or four lectures to ideas in that realm. Lecturer B may think humanistic psychology is mush and not say a word about it, or only a critical word in passing, but may be quite excited about the five-factor trait theory of personality. The students of the two instructors hear different content, but in a more important sense they have similar experiences. They all experience the genuine, passionate, critical thinking of a scholar who values students sufficiently to share his or her thoughts and excitement with them.

A textbook is typically and properly more conservative than a set of lectures. In an idea-based textbook, the author is clearly present as a thinking human being, but the particular passions and viewpoints of the author are more muted than is the case for lectures. The textbook's foremost task is to present psychology as it is collectively construed by the diverse people who make up the discipline. A good textbook for an idea-centered course has an interesting narrative and a focus on ideas, but it is also a reference book, which sets forth the full range of psychology. During the development of any major introductory textbook, drafts of each chapter are critically reviewed by experts in that chapter's realm, including experts deliberately chosen because their viewpoints differ from the author's. Publishers put textbooks through that process because a book that diverges too widely from standard topics and opinions will not sell. The result is a more balanced presentation of each realm of psychology than most authors would otherwise produce.

Precisely because of its conservative nature, a good textbook is a liberating tool for the lecturer in an idea-centered course. Because the textbook covers standard ground, the lecturer is free to veer from the standard. The lecturer can develop unconventional ideas that are not in the textbook at all or (more often) develop fully ideas that are only touched on in the book. The lecturer can also argue with the textbook, pointing out weaknesses in its development of an idea and introducing alternative interpretations. In doing that, the lecturer not only presents an alternative view concerning a particular idea but also inspires students to read more thoughtfully and critically themselves.

A difficulty that stems from textbooks' tendency toward all-inclusive coverage is that most contain too much for the typical one-semester course. Instructors need not assign the whole book, however. Chapters can be left out or, better yet, pared down by letting students know which ideas in each chapter are fair game for the test.

The most common mistake that introductory psychology instructors make, in my opinion, is that of becoming slaves to the textbook. Many assume they must cover in lectures everything they assign in the textbook or it is not fair game on the test; conversely, many assume that nothing said in lectures is fair game unless it also appears in the book. A great liberation occurs when the instructor realizes that both of these assumptions are false. Students can read a textbook with understanding if it is well written; they can also listen in class and take notes if the lecture is clear; and they do both of these if they know that the test includes ideas and evidence from both sources. My own formula, stated on the course syllabus, is that 70% of the points on each test are based on the textbook and 30% are based on lectures.

TESTS THAT CALL FOR REASONS AND EVIDENCE

Tests, unfortunately, are the tail that wags the dog of nearly every college course, idea centered or not. We have arranged the educational system in such a way that students see their goal as that of achieving a high grade, whether or not such achievement reflects learning that is worthwhile for any other end. If we want students to think about the ideas presented in lectures and readings, we must test in a way that rewards such thought. That is especially challenging in large classes, where, realistically, tests must be objectively scorable.

In my experience, the best objective test questions in idea-centered courses are those that ask about the reasoning or evidence that was given for or against a particular idea. Rather than ask what Freud believed, I ask what reasons Freud offered in support of one of his beliefs. Rather than ask which of two theories was supported by a particular study, I ask what result supported one theory over another. When students know they will be tested on reasons and evidence, they attend to those as they listen to lectures and read the textbook, and such attention tends to promote thought. The best way by far to encode reasons and evidence into memory for a future test is to think about them.

Such questions can be presented in multiple-choice form. For instance, a particular test item might state an idea that had been discussed in a lecture or in the textbook and then ask the students to select, from a set of choices, a fact or finding that had been presented in support of that idea. Such questions are usually longer, and take longer for students to read and answer, than conventional multiple-choice questions. My 50-minute tests for a large class typically consist of 25 multiple-choice questions and three short essay questions (selected by students from a set of four). Early in the course I let students know, with examples, the kinds of questions I ask, so they know how to take notes in class and how to study their textbook.

WRITING ASSIGNMENTS THAT PROMOTE CRITICAL THOUGHT

Writing assignments in an idea-centered course should be explicitly oriented toward inducing critical thought about ideas. In my experience, the typical term paper assignment—in which students are asked to write about some general topic based on library research—is effective only in small classes where the instructor critiques successive drafts or requires students to defend their papers in an oral discussion. Otherwise, most students write term papers with very little thought. Through a rather random process they locate books or articles on their topic, read parts of them somewhat randomly, and write a paper summarizing or paraphrasing what they read, sometimes not even understanding what they have written. In my experience, pointed writing assignments can induce thought much more effectively than general term papers.

Critiquing the Textbook's Citation

I have found the following assignment to be especially effective. Ask students to identify an idea in their textbook that seems particularly interesting to them and that the author supports by referring to a particular research study. Ask them to look up that study in the library, read it to see if it really does support the idea that the author claims it does, and write a brief paper answering the following three questions: (a) What claim did the textbook author make in citing the study? (b) What was actually done in the study and what was found? and (c) Do the results actually support the claim made by the textbook author, and why or why not?

I used to give that assignment regularly before I had written my own textbook, and my students and I had great fun with it at the expense of textbook authors. I no longer use the assignment now that I am using my own textbook, because the one time I tried it my students were too gentle in their criticisms. I strongly recommend it, however, to anyone who is not a textbook author. The assignment requires students to focus attention on an idea and the evidence offered, to find a journal in the library, to read a research study critically to answer a particular question, to think about the adequacy of evidence, and to write conclusions and reasons clearly. In the process, some students also develop a healthy skepticism about claims in textbooks. In a small class, or in a class divided into small discussion groups, students can be asked to share their findings with each other orally.

If you try the assignment, be sure to warn students that they may have to go through several different articles (and ideas in the textbook) before they come to an article that is available in the library and is understandable to them. They do not have to understand everything in the article, but they must understand the methods and results well enough to answer the questions with some confidence. Supplying students with a list of the psychology journals in the school's library helps them narrow down their potential selections from the textbook's references and spares them some frustration. You should also explain the difference between empirical articles and review articles and ask students to use only the former. Ask students to staple a photocopy of the journal article to their paper, so you or your grading assistant can skim it to see if their interpretation is reasonable.

Question Essays

Another valuable assignment, which I have long used, is to ask students to write out, in brief essay form, questions that were stimulated by their reading of each chapter of the textbook. When I first tried this assignment I was disappointed by the results. The questions were superficial, or seemingly irrelevant to anything in the chapter, or clearly answered in the chapter, or so poorly stated that I could not make sense of them. Moreover, some students complained that they had no questions because they "understood everything in the chapter." I now make the point of the assignment clear, and offer guidance, by giving students a sheet containing the following instructions:

> To think is to question. If you read your textbook thoughtfully, questions will come continuously to your mind. Sometimes a concept or idea will not make sense to you. Sometimes it will make sense, but you will disagree with it. Sometimes you will wonder about the evidence for the idea, or about its possible applications to real life. All such thoughts can be framed as questions. As you read, jot down—in abbreviated form, in the margin of your textbook—some of the questions that come to your mind. As you read along, you may find the answers to some of your questions. Cross off the answered ones. By the time you have completed the chapter you will have jotted down many questions. Go back and read those questions and think about them. Cross off any that you now can answer or that no longer seem very interesting.
>
> From the questions that remain, select three and write them out in a more elaborate form to be handed in. Each of these must come from a different major section of the chapter (there are typically three to five major sections in each chapter). Each question should be written in the form of a brief essay (several sentences) and may come from any of the following three categories:
>
> 1. *Honest difficulty understanding something.* Some seemingly important idea discussed in the chapter is not clear, even though you have tried hard to understand it. In elaborating on this kind of question begin by indicating what you do understand about the idea and then specify as clearly as possible what you don't understand. If you think you might understand it but are not sure, state in your own words what you think to be the case and indicate why you are not sure.
>
> 2. *Questioning the material (disagreement, challenge, or requests for further evidence).* Here you understand clearly the point that the author (or the person whose idea is being described) is making, but you are not sure you agree with it. Begin by stating succinctly the idea you are questioning, and then indicate why you are questioning it. What leads you to think the idea might be wrong? What kind of evidence would convince you one way or the other about this point?
>
> 3. *Questions that go beyond the material.* Here something in the chapter has stimulated you to ask a question that goes beyond the scope of the chapter. For example, you might wonder if a particular phenomenon described in the chapter would apply under conditions that are not described. Begin by indicating the idea that stimulated your question and then state the question. Then you might propose a possible answer and indicate the kind of evidence that would allow you to determine if your answer is correct.
>
> . . . Question sets will be graded as follows: 0 = didn't do it, or just scribbled something down, or handed it in late; 1 = ques-

tions do not reflect careful reading and thought, or are sloppily written, or are difficult to understand; 2 = questions indicate that you have read the chapter, given the ideas some thought, and have taken some care in writing; 3 = questions reflect a careful reading of the chapter, are thoughtful and thought provoking, and are well written.

Even with these instructions many students find the assignment hard at the beginning, and some complain about it. Reading this way seems awkward to them; they do not automatically form questions as they read. With time and persistence, however, most students become better at it. At the end of the semester about three fourths of the class typically say, on an anonymous questionnaire, that the assignment helped them read more thoughtfully and critically. The remaining one fourth seems to include two categories—those who did not need the assignment because they already read thoughtfully and those who never really tried the assignment as it was described but continued to read in an unquestioning manner and to make up perfunctory questions afterward (for which they usually received a low grade).

In my course, the students bring their questions each week to their small discussion group meetings (each led by an undergraduate teaching assistant), where each student reads aloud at least one of his or her questions and some of them lead to extended discussion. That gives the questions a clear purpose beyond encouraging an active mode of reading, which helps motivate students to put effort into the assignment. The most common complaint about the assignment after the first few weeks in the semester is that too many of the questions never get answered. I interpret that complaint positively; the questions are apparently genuine. I do try to answer in class some questions that call for clarification of ideas or evidence in the book, especially if the same question was asked by many students; occasionally I devote a whole lecture to a particularly fascinating question that extends beyond what was in the book. Some students, on the course evaluation, express pleasure that one of their own questions helped shape the course content despite the large class size.

Helping Students Meet the Challenge

To meet the challenge of the idea-centered course, some students need extra help. They do not need help of the typical tutorial kind, in which explanations given in the textbook or lectures are simply rephrased.

Rather, they need help in learning to read and listen actively, so as to identify ideas and think about arguments and evidence.

The students who need the most help are those who—despite the idea-centered format of the lectures, readings, writing assignments, and tests—do not shake themselves loose of their passive study methods. In lectures they write down, verbatim, the lecture idea and some of the facts and term definitions, but they somehow miss the argument that connects all of these. They read (or look through) the textbook pages with highlighter in hand, yellowing sentences that contain bold-faced terms or that look, for other reasons, like they might appear on the test. The night before the test they rehearse their notebook statements and the highlighted passages in their textbook, or worse, they rehearse the even more condensed and atomized versions of these that they have copied out onto a review list. Their goal is to memorize each item sufficiently to recognize it in a multiple-choice question or reproduce it in a written-answer question. Such methods may get them through other college courses but are completely ineffective in an idea-centered course.

TECHNIQUES FOR READING AND LISTENING

The techniques that I have found to be most helpful in encouraging active, thoughtful reading and listening were developed by Marcia Heiman, who for several years directed a learning program at Boston College and Roxbury Community College. In controlled experiments at the two institutions, high-risk students who were taught her techniques achieved higher grade point averages and withdrew from fewer courses than did similar students who received standard subject-matter tutorials or no special help (Heiman, 1987). The techniques apparently help students in all courses, even those that test primarily for term definitions and specific facts; but they are especially valuable for idea-centered courses. I teach these techniques to students who seek extra help, and I require them to show evidence that they are using the techniques if they want to continue to get help from me or a graduate teaching assistant.

Inferring the Author's Questions

Heiman observed that students often miss the main ideas or arguments in their readings because they focus too narrowly on the details and see each as a separate capsule of information. To help broaden their focus, she insists that they read with a pen or pencil in hand, not a highlighter, and that they write certain questions and notes in the margin as they read. Their most basic task is to identify the question or questions that the author is attempting to answer in each section of a chapter. In many books the questions are implicit, and students who do not infer them have no chance of understanding the purpose of the various facts and arguments presented. Heiman requires students to infer and write out each of the author's questions in the textbook margin and to circle passages and make notes that point to the author's answer and reasoning.

I modify Heiman's technique in applying it to my own textbook, because in that book my questions are stated explicitly, as numbered focus questions in the margin next to the relevant paragraphs. Most of the questions have to do with evidence for or applications of larger ideas developed in the chapter. I suggest to all students that they read each question before reading the adjacent paragraphs and that they read the paragraphs specifically to answer the question. For students who need extra help I reinforce this by insisting that they write notes in the margins summarizing the answers to each question. I also ask them to come to their meetings with me or the teaching assistant prepared to restate the focus questions in their own words and to answer them with the help of their notes.

Inferring the Lecturer's Questions

Heiman's advice for taking notes in lectures is similar to that for reading. She tells students that to understand a lecture they must figure out what question or questions the lecturer is trying to answer and then must follow the path of the answer. She requires students to create a wide left-hand margin (about 1/3 page wide) on each of their notebook pages, to write their lecture notes only to the right of the margin, and to write in the margin the questions they believe the lecturer is trying to answer and their own comments or questions concerning the lecturer's answer. At first many students fill in the margin after class, because they cannot both write down what the lecturer is saying and think about it at the same time; but with practice most find that they can identify the questions and route to answering it as they listen. As they learn to think while listening and writing, they become better at separating the wheat from the chaff and more selective in their note taking.

The process of identifying explicitly the author's and lecturer's questions, answers, and reasons helps students become more critical in their reading and listening. Sometimes they find that an author's or lecturer's question is unclear, or is clear but not answered, or is answered but the answer is not supported with logic or evidence. When students begin to complain or to ask questions of their own based on such observations, they are beginning to behave as scholars.

In an idea-centered course the lecturer is not defensive about such questions and complaints but accepts them as prods to become more clear and logical.

TECHNIQUES FOR REVIEWING FOR TESTS

Students who do poorly in an idea-centered course commonly review material by abstracting pieces of information from their textbook and notebook onto separate review lists, which they then attempt to commit to memory. In producing such lists, they typically miss the larger ideas and arguments that connect the pieces together. Because they subsequently study only from their abstracted notes, they have no chance later of discovering the ideas and arguments they missed originally.

Using the Margin Questions and Notes as a Review Guide

I advise students to prepare for tests primarily by going through their textbook chapters and lecture notes again, with the aim of identifying each idea and the arguments and evidence pertaining to it. The author's or lecturer's questions in the margins are the beginning points for such review. The student rereads each question and tries to reconstruct the author's or lecturer's answer and evidence pertaining to it, with or without the aid of the additional marginal comments and textual circlings that had been made earlier. Whenever the student cannot reconstruct an argument from memory, he or she need only read the original paragraphs adjacent to the margin notes and make new notes concerning the argument. In this way, students can find and think about the ideas and arguments that they missed in their original reading.

Hierarchical Summary Charts

In addition to studying from the original pages, many students find it useful to condense the information from many pages of text down to a single page. Such a condensation, if properly done, can help them see the larger picture and lines of connection among more specific items of information. For this purpose, I teach students how to make hierarchical summary charts, which are quite different from the lists that many of them would make on their own.

An example of such a chart, which summarizes one section of the memory chapter of my textbook, appears in Figure 1. The top node refers to the large idea to which the whole section is devoted (in this case, the idea that some strategies are better than others for encoding information into long-term memory). The second level of nodes pre-

FIGURE 1

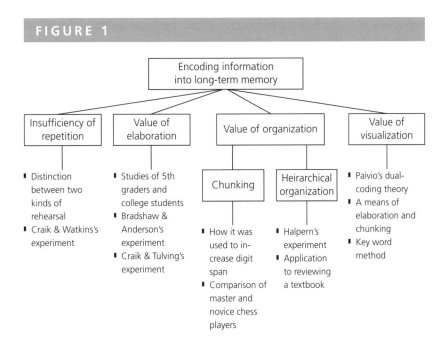

Sample hierarchical summary chart, which summarizes the ideas, evidence, and applications presented in one major section of a textbook chapter on memory. Students can create such charts to summarize large amounts of information in a manner that preserves the logical connections among the various items. From *Psychology,* 2nd ed. (p. 341), by P. Gray, 1994, New York: Worth. Copyright 1994 by Worth. Adapted with permission.

sents the more specific ideas pertaining to the larger idea (in this case, to the value of particular encoding strategies). The bulleted points underneath these nodes refer to specific lines of evidence for, and applications of, the second-level ideas.

Such charts are easier for students to sketch out than they might at first seem. Textbooks are organized hierarchically; major headings reflect broad ideas, and subordinate headings reflect more specific ideas that pertain to the broad ones. The boxed nodes of Figure 1, in fact, correspond precisely to the headings that appear in the chapter section being summarized, and the bulleted points correspond with the specific studies and applications developed underneath each heading. In creating such a chart, students must focus attention on the logic of the author's organization, which can help them immensely in following the arguments. The chart is a useful tool for review because it summarizes, on one easily visualized page, all of the information that appears on many pages of text, in a manner that preserves the connections among ideas, evidence, and applications. Typically, three to six such charts suffice to summarize an entire textbook chapter. I devote part of a lecture to teaching all students how to make such charts, and I require students who come for extra help to show me that they are in fact making them.

Conclusion

In this chapter I have described the general goal of idea-centered teaching and some specific means for achieving that goal. The means include lectures that focus explicitly on ideas and arguments; the complementary rather than redundant use of lectures and textbook; tests that focus on reasons and evidence; writing assignments that promote thought rather than regurgitation; and specific techniques to help students focus their attention on ideas and evidence as they read their textbook, listen to lectures, and review for tests. These are not the only possible means to the desired end, which is to promote students' intellectual engagement and critical thought with and about psychology, but they work well in my experience. I encourage you to try some of them if you have not already or to use them as mental prods to develop other means that may work even better for you and your students.

References

Gray, P. (1993). Engaging students' intellects: The immersion approach to critical thinking in psychology instruction. *Teaching of Psychology, 20,* 68–74.

Gray, P. (1994). *Psychology* (2nd ed.). New York: Worth.

Gray, P. (1996). Incorporating evolutionary theory into the teaching of psychology. *Teaching of Psychology, 23,* 207–214.

Heiman, M. (1987). Learning to learn: A behavioral approach to improved thinking. In D. N. Perkins, J. Lochhead, & J. Bishop (Eds.), *Thinking: The second international conference* (pp. 431–452). Hillsdale, NJ: Erlbaum.

Prawat, R. S. (1991). The value of ideas: The immersion approach to the development of thinking. *Educational Researcher, 20*(2), 3–10.

Lester A. Lefton

Why I Teach the Way I Do:
Repackaging Psychology

4

have had many a waiter, lawyer, or salesperson come up to me and ask, "You're Professor Lefton, aren't you?" Like most other instructors in a university town, I often run into former students from my introductory psychology classes. After a brief awkwardness, I usually ask how they enjoyed the class and what they remember about psychology. Another brief silence ensues, and then I invariably get post-course feedback on their experience and their retention of various facts or ideas. The sample of students is admittedly small, nonrepresentative, and biased (often by their efforts to please me with their prodigious memories). Nevertheless, I have been able to learn through these chance encounters a great deal about teaching psychology.

My former students sometimes remember a joke, a particularly vivid example, or a demonstration. But more often they tell me about studies of dreams, prejudice, or depression—topics that interest them personally. What I pay particular attention to, though, is the extent to which former students remember basic principles of psychology. I work hard to teach the principles—key ideas and organizing themes, which I hope students will take with them and be able to use for a lifetime—in a meaningful, easy-to-remember way.

I design my class and my textbook according to certain guiding principles. I try to (a) be selective in what I teach; (b) adapt to my students' learning styles; (c) teach critical thinking and learning strategies; (d) work from application to theory; (e) help students recognize and be sensitive to issues of diversity, including age, gender, and ethnicity; (f) keep the course current and exciting; (g) engage students; and (h) teach psychology as a unified, coherent discipline.

Be Selective

Our discipline has grown in extraordinary ways. The depth of psychology has continued to expand through new theoretical insights, new biological discoveries, and greater understanding of the environment's role in shaping behavior and mental processes. The breadth of the discipline has expanded as well. No longer dominated by a few topics, psychology now requires that we understand, study, and explore the full range of human behaviors, including imagery, thought, health, environment, sports, community, peace, religion, and neurobiology, to name but a few. With the field having grown so enormously, how can we teach it within one semester, or even two? In some ways, the task for each of us has become nearly impossible.

Instructors feel that they must teach innumerable complicated facts, people, and concepts. As a consequence, they often get bogged down describing a specific study or application, and other important ideas are inadvertently left out. Herein lies the balancing act—depth of coverage versus breadth of coverage. True, students have to be taught about classical conditioning, instrumental conditioning, and observational learning. But how long should we spend on each topic? How much depth should we explore? What topics dare we skip?

I can prescribe what I think are the key ideas of psychology. And they are likely to be similar to those that most instructors think are important. But, my specific course outline is not so important. It is far more crucial for instructors to develop their own action plans. Each instructor then has to decide the key themes, ideas, and concepts that allow their students to have a good introductory grasp of psychology.

I believe that in the introductory course, we are not trying to prepare preprofessionals. They do not need to know or be taught all that has ever been thought about or researched before. Students do, however, need to understand the depth, breadth, complexity, and excitement of our science. They also need to be able to read, listen to, and interpret information presented to them through the media, in other courses, and in their day-to-day interactions in the world.

As instructors, our 45 hours with students are not enough; so we ask students to read textbooks and other material to round out what we teach. As a textbook author, I rely on my text to fill the gaps that I cannot cover in class. I assume students will do the reading and see how my classroom views are complemented by—and sometimes differ from—views expressed in the text. To a great extent, one's textbook selection allows one's classroom goals to be met. An accessible but comprehensive text allows an instructor to focus on the key ideas because the instructor knows that the supporting ideas, facts, theories, and controversies are presented and evaluated elsewhere.

Adapt to Today's Students

Most instructors lay out the facts, theories, controversies, and applications for students. They may provide handouts, overheads, outlines, and key terms and issues in an organized, coherent, and straightforward manner. Like a well-organized tour of a museum, they may walk students through a course, moving from learning to memory to the other cognitive processes; studying abnormality leads to an examination of diagnostic systems, as well as to studies of treatment.

Yet many instructors are beginning to realize that today's students do not always learn in the linear, guided mode to which instructors may have been accustomed. Some students organize their discovery of knowledge by working backward from the endpoint. Others skip from topic to topic (Piaget at noon, Bandura at one o'clock). Far too many don't have a strategy at all. For those instructors who take to technology, the use of CD-ROMs, video disks, and interactive media is often a help for students with alternative learning styles.

Encourage Critical Thinking

By helping students acquire critical learning strategies, we help students learn not only psychology but also how to succeed in life. We nurture critical thinking skills by using teaching strategies that emphasize research, applications, cultural diversity, and the scientific method. Learning specific facts is important, but placing those facts within a context is far more important. Teaching students to understand the scientific reasoning process and to draw conclusions and make decisions based on reasonable assumptions and well-drawn hypotheses is an essential aspect of teaching the introductory course. In my course and in my text, I present research in ways that allow students to critically evaluate it and to draw their own conclusions. From time to time in each I also ask several focused questions to encourage critical thinking. These questions suggest new ideas and perspectives for students to consider as they evaluate the research studies presented. At the end of each major unit, I ask students to make connections between topics spanning the course. These are not the only places in the course where they should use their critical thinking skills, but they are places where I ask them to be especially evaluative.

Work From Application to Theory

In my classroom and in my text, I try to work from application to theory. By this I mean that I often pose a question to students about a real-life situation and ask them to ponder out loud, sometimes in writing, the key variables, central issues, and further applications of the situation. For example, in a unit on developmental psychology, it is easy to begin by asking students what they think are the implications of day care for society. Even students who hadn't previously thought about this issue are quick to discern many of the important variables. In a large class, there are usually a wide range of opinions as to the efficacy of day care or the negative implications of day care for intellectual and social development. After the students have worked through all of these issues, I formally present attachment theory, introduce Piaget's theories of intellectual development, Vygotsky's ideas, and studies of moral development. I then raise the child care issue again, but I add now the question, "What would Bowlby, Piaget, Vygotsky, Kohlberg, and Gilligan have to say about these issues?" By forcing students to think within the context of applications, theory begins to make more sense.

Although one course goal is to teach the facts of attachment theory, as well as Piaget's theory of intellectual development, a more important goal is to have students remember the central ideas of psychology. This is best done within the context of applications that are meaningful and through which students can see the world from their own vantage points. A student from a lower socioeconomic background will view the issue of day care differently from an individual for whom finances are less important. By combining research, theory, and application into a meaningful unit, all students will have conceptual pegs on which to hang the issues.

Recognize Diversity

One need not be a futurist to realize that the demographic complexity of the United States is changing extraordinarily rapidly. The ethnic and racial complexion of our country by the year 2030 will look very different from the way it looks today. We will be an older society, one with many more people of color, with a workforce composed of more women and minorities. We know, for example, that in the 1980s, the non-Hispanic White population grew by less than 8% (the African American population increased by 13% to 30 million), but the Hispanic American population grew by 53% to 23 million. Psychology is strengthened by understanding rather than avoiding the range of people's interests, views, and abilities. Research and theory become more complete when the multicultural nature of human beings is explored.

On a more practical level, the helping professions are enhanced when practitioners understand their clients. For example, Asian American families have strongly held views about respect for elders and the continuity of the family. Asian American culture, like any culture, helps its group members interpret what they have seen, felt, and experienced; it offers guidelines for interpreting the world. Furthermore, we know that more than half of the people seen by mental health practitioners are women, but this may be because men with mental health problems are less likely to seek therapy. These differences must be explored to find their causes. The variety of psychologists, their research interests, and their socioeconomic and ethnic backgrounds are now contributing to a greater recognition of diversity among people—and this diversity is a strength that psychologists today not only recognize but should also celebrate.

Keep the Course Current and Exciting

Psychology is a fast-changing field with constantly new findings. For instructors this is both a challenge and a treat. Instructors cannot rely on 20-year-old notes and old-fashioned demonstrations. Students know when an instructor's interest has waned to this extent. Within milliseconds, they can discern a lack of desire, excitement, and involvement with the topic. Today's students require and demand a contemporary course that is up-to-date and accurate.

We all know that the media provide a barrage of information about new psychological discoveries. The information they present is often inaccurate or incomplete—and this can be an opening for instructors to show the complexity and dynamism of psychology. Use these incomplete, sloppy news reports and glib generalizations to reveal the complexities of psychology. Have students go to the library and find the original scientific articles on which news reports are based; let them dissect the articles in class. This will show the complexity of research, demonstrate the wide number of variables that are usually involved, and provide an opportunity to keep the class especially current. (Even instructors who do not have library resources can find an article in the newspaper, do an interlibrary loan, and have both available before class—a little less spontaneous, but equally effective.)

The use of popular press reports—and their lack of scientific rigor—is a great opportunity to keep lectures spirited and to show an instructor's continuing interest, excitement, and desire. That excitement is infectious, and it will teach students to act like investigative reporters when reading and thinking about scientific issues.

Engage Students

Engaging students intellectually is a key goal. Yet the way this is accomplished involves a tension between teaching popular, interesting, and (potentially) important topics versus teaching fundamental ideas that all instructors know are central to understanding psychology. Working from application to theory helps. Using popular media reports also helps. But more than any other specific technique, the instructor's *voice*—his or her views, opinions, and approach—can make the real difference. A good course has a clear voice. This is sometimes the voice of a clinician. Sometimes it is the voice of a skeptic, a methodologist, or perhaps a biologically trained researcher. If an instructor's voice is clear, unambiguous, and nevertheless balanced in its presentation, it makes for an opportunity to capture students.

Engaging students sometimes means being provocative and putting your personality out front; other times it means walking them slowly and systematically through a difficult concept. Each instructor will have his or her own way of doing this: modulating one's voice, taking strong viewpoints, demonstrating difficult ideas and concepts, asking students to keep journals. Finding ways to help students generate personal meaning from the material, to involve them intellectually and emotionally in the science of psychology, is not only challenging but it also makes teaching fun.

Teach a Unified Discipline

When our discipline was founded, its theoreticians were trained in philosophy, medicine, physics, and education. They brought their expertise to bear on understanding human behavior and thought. As many have argued, psychology has always been caught between the dialectic tension of wanting to know more and more about less and less or less and less about more and more (e.g., Fowler, 1990). We need to emphasize the whole picture while at the same time examining the details. To a certain extent, we must teach psychology as a unified whole discipline made up of parts, lest we encourage our students to see us as a fragmented science with a distance between our knowledge base and our profession. The cooperative interdependence of application and theory, science and speculation, teaching and research should be our goal.

In 1969 George Miller wrote an influential article in which he suggested that we have to "give psychology away," meaning essentially that psychologists need to make their knowledge and findings accessible to the public. Over the past three decades, we have been providing data and theory to each other and to the public at an increasingly rapid pace. I recently attended a conference of department chairs in which Charles Brewer (1995) suggested that we have to take psychology back. It is Brewer's argument that we have been giving away too many facts, too many theories, and too much unintegrated information. In many ways, I agree. Giving psychology away as a series of discrete packages of information adds little to students' powers of analysis. We need to package our information in meaningful units that will be remembered, analyzed, and thought about critically. This requires selectivity, adaptability, critical analysis, application of theory, recognition of diversity, and a current, engaging course. That's why I teach the way I do.

References

Brewer, C. (1995, December). *Let's take back psychology*. Paper presented at the meeting of the Association of Heads of Departments of Psychology, Southeastern Psychological Association, Atlanta, GA.

Fowler, R. D. (1990). Psychology: The core discipline. *American Psychologist, 45,* 1–6.

Miller, G. A. (1969). Psychology as a means of promoting human welfare. *American Psychologist, 24,* 1063–1075.

Margaret W. Matlin

Distilling Psychology Into 700 Pages:

Some Goals for Writing an Introductory Psychology Textbook

5

ntroductory psychology is a course that encourages us to capture all the passions, ambitions, paradoxes, and atrocities of the human condition. How could such a stunning variety of individuals all represent the same species?

I began to write this chapter on a Thursday in the second week of the fall semester. The stories I heard on that day were probably representative of the kinds of issues we address in introductory psychology. One student—with a grade point average of 3.9 and Graduate Record Examination scores above 1,500—came to my office to ask what else he might do to improve his chances of being admitted to his first-choice graduate program. In my course in cognitive psychology, I asked students for examples of flashbulb memories ... and then remembered that one student had recently separated from an abusive husband. Her flashbulb memories were certainly more painfully vivid than the impersonal examples of national tragedies that most of us remember. A student from introductory psychology shyly passed me a note after class. In a previous assignment on confounding variables in everyday decision making, she had written about how she had been crying each day from homesickness. I had jotted a letter to her, suggesting other ways she could reinterpret her new experiences; fortunately, her note back to me reassured me that her outlook was now much more positive.

When I returned home from classes on that Thursday, my daughter Sally showed me the notes she had just prepared on some interviews she had conducted with children and their families in rural Nicaragua:

> Angel and Enrique haven't attended school lately because they have no notebooks or paper, but their mother is grateful that the family of 10 has enough to eat almost every day. In another family, Maria Luisa (age 8) is very interested in school, but she and her brother Adonis (age 7) often cannot attend because they have nothing to eat and they don't have notebooks, pencils, or clothing.

These testimonies reminded me that the life stories of North American students may often be sad or even tragic, but they seldom approach the struggles of individuals in developing countries.

Introductory psychology is the only course that attempts to explore the wide scope of these human experiences. Moreover—as if this goal were not sufficient—introductory psychology must also examine our basic psychological abilities to perceive, learn, remember, think, and talk.

For me, the prime incentive to write a textbook was the luxury of providing a more comprehensive story of humanity than had been possible in my earlier writing projects. In my first textbook, *Human Experimental Psychology* (Matlin, 1979), I had enjoyed telling students about research techniques and encouraging them to develop the critical thinking tools that are necessary to analyze the flawed conclusions we draw in everyday interactions. My textbooks *Sensation and Perception* (Matlin & Foley, 1997) and *Cognition* (Matlin, in press) explore vitally important topics in psychology, though the media may not consider them startling enough to include on Oprah Winfrey's show. I am hopeful, however, that the more motivated students in these two disciplines will develop a sense of wonder about some of the interesting questions in these fields. For example, how does the visual system provide for size constancy? What would be a logical way to classify the various smells in olfactory research? Under what conditions can we gather information about an unattended message? Why are older children more effective than younger children in recalling material?

When I wrote a textbook called *The Psychology of Women* (Matlin, 1996), I crossed the boundary. Those previous textbooks described, and I hope that they also stimulated curiosity or even admiration for, our perceptual and cognitive "equipment." However, the psychology of women is a topic that provokes emotional reactions. It encourages both women and men to examine their values: "What really matters in my life? Should I strive to become a leader in my profession? Does my love relationship matter more than my career? Will I have the time and energy to be a good parent, when I have all these other goals?"

This discipline also explores controversies, such as attitudes toward lesbians and gay males, affirmative action, and abortion. It also presents depressing information about wage gaps, health problems, incest, rape, sexual harassment, battering, psychological disorders, and impoverished elderly women.

Writing *The Psychology of Women* stimulated my enthusiasm for developing a more comprehensive overview of psychology. I had taught introductory psychology for 10 years at this point, and I enjoyed having considerable expertise in large chunks of the discipline. Most topics in the beginning of the introductory psychology course were very familiar from my textbooks in experimental psychology, sensation and perception, and cognitive psychology. My textbook in psychology of women had provided perspectives on important topics in developmental psychology, motivation, psychological disorders and their treatment, social psychology, and health psychology. Furthermore, my graduate work with Bob Zajonc at Michigan had supplied additional perspectives on social psychology. However, I felt less familiar with topics such as biological psychology, consciousness, emotion, and assessment, as well as with areas within clinical psychology and health psychology that were not relevant to gender.

In summary, a major motivator for my decision to write an introductory psychology textbook was to understand more about the Big Picture, to try to fit together some new pieces into the jigsaw puzzle. I have always relished large-scale projects, and every contributor to this book would agree that writing an introductory psychology textbook is definitely a large-scale project!

In writing the introductory textbook, I was amazed at the drastic change in the scope of the lenses with which I began to view the world. When writing a textbook in experimental psychology, I went through life noticing how research could be flawed and how we often draw erroneous conclusions in our daily lives. My sensory and perceptual world becomes vibrantly alive during each revision of the *Sensation and Perception* textbook. I recently finished revising the psychology of women textbook, and gender seemed to permeate the media, personal interactions, and every professional article I read. I have just completed the fourth edition of the *Cognition* textbook. Therefore, examples of human memory, problem solving, and decision making are thrust into the foreground. However, once one takes on a textbook in introductory psychology, the world does not look the same. Every aspect of human behavior is now relevant!

In this chapter, I begin by discussing my approach to teaching introductory psychology to college undergraduates. Then I consider how these goals can be expanded in writing a textbook for introductory psychology.

Philosophy for Teaching Introductory Psychology in the Classroom

When we teach introductory psychology, we are forced to examine our goals by asking questions we do not ask for our other courses. After all, only a fraction of our students become psychology majors; most pursue careers in sales, law, medicine, education, computer science, the arts, and other areas that we psychologists tend to neglect. This course in introductory psychology is our only opportunity to reach these students and to persuade them that a knowledge of psychological principles can enrich their personal lives, improve their performance in the workplace, and make them more effective human beings. However, this course must also provide a solid academic background for those students who (like ourselves) find that psychology is overwhelmingly appealing and become psychology majors.

Several years ago, Drew Appleby developed Project Syllabus for Division 2 of the American Psychological Association. This project assembles model syllabi for a variety of courses. One of Drew's criteria for an effective course syllabus was that it should specify the instructor's goals for the course. After all, students should know what the professor hopes to accomplish during the term. This criterion challenged me to transform my general thoughts about the purpose of teaching introductory psychology into more carefully articulated objectives. For the past two semesters, my syllabus has described the following four major goals for my students:

1. An appreciation for the important concepts of psychology, including both research and theory. You will discover that this information is more complex than the simple summaries often provided by the popular media.
2. An ability to evaluate psychological research more critically, so that you know whether to trust the material you read about psychology after you complete this course. To enhance your critical thinking skills, you will need to understand information about psychological research.
3. An ability to apply your knowledge to everyday situations such as studying more effectively for exams, understanding some general approaches to psychotherapy, and appreciating how to help resolve conflicts.
4. An appreciation for human diversity, accompanied by the understanding that the characteristics we all share are more

important than the differences that often threaten to separate us.

These goals guide me when I review my plan for teaching introductory psychology before the beginning of each semester. For example, if I sincerely believe that students must understand research methods, then I must discuss this topic throughout the course, not simply in the second lecture of the term. I am always on the lookout, for example, for a social psychology study that illustrates the experimental method, and we can discuss why some feature—such as random assignment—is necessary or how the researchers took certain ethical precautions. If one of my goals is to emphasize diversity, then my discussion of psychotherapy should not assume that all clients are White. Instead, we might explore some of the problems that Asian Americans might experience when they seek therapy.

I have taught psychology courses for 25 years, and my style of teaching has evolved. During my first experiences in the classroom, I adopted a "banker" model, primarily interested in depositing information in students' heads (Matlin, 1995a). My lectures did emphasize clarity and organization, but I was not especially interested in engaging my students. In retrospect, my emphasis was perfectly understandable; my professors at Stanford and Michigan had almost all been bankers. Soon, however, my lecture style evolved, and I realized that students could learn much more effectively if I included numerous examples and related the material to everyday experiences.

With the recent emphasis on active learning (e.g., Andreoli-Mathie, 1993; Nodine, 1994), my philosophy of teaching in the classroom has evolved further. I now am more likely to have students write short summaries of a topic, discuss an issue with the person sitting next to them, or do something else to become actively engaged with the material. I design discussion questions for the whole class, and I let students know that their own questions are very welcome. I enjoy the sense of community that can evolve in a classroom, the sense of a caring bond between the professor and students. In summary, my aim is to make the introductory psychology classroom as interactive as possible while also emphasizing my four content-related goals.

In writing an introductory psychology textbook, I focus on the same four goals that are central in my classroom. In the remainder of this chapter, I address an important responsibility of any textbook author—writing clearly. Then I examine how my approach emphasizes the four central goals of conveying content, encouraging critical thinking, applying psychology in everyday life, and addressing human diversity.

Writing Clearly

Obviously, a textbook cannot carry on a two-way conversation with students in the same way that a professor can in the classroom. However, a primary goal when I write textbooks is to try to present material in a clear and engaging fashion, with examples and applications. Whenever I write, I imagine myself in the classroom, trying to convey the particular concept. This process keeps me honest. If my description is too abstract or too complex, I can visualize my students gazing out the window, doodling in their notebooks, or looking absolutely lost. I can also picture their puzzled expressions if my transition between topics is too abrupt or my overall organization is too subtle. Furthermore, I can sense when my students would need me to pause and briefly review before moving on.

Authors must write each paragraph in a clear and well-organized fashion, but they also have a responsibility to students to provide overall structure to the discipline. Fortunately, introductory psychology is a course that already has a fairly well established sequence of chapters. (The issue of topic order is far more challenging in a discipline such as psychology of women.) I try to provide additional structure in all my books by developing three to five themes for each book. These themes may not be particularly novel or surprising, but they encourage students to see consistent patterns throughout a discipline. I also try to point out connections between chapters that might initially seem unrelated. For example, the same schemas that operate when we try to remember words also operate when we try to remember people's personal characteristics. A learning principle that students mastered in chapter 6 may be applied to psychotherapy in chapter 15. An overarching goal is to provide a coherent framework for an introductory subject that might otherwise seem like a banquet of hors d'oeuvres.

My knowledge of cognitive psychology forces me to emphasize pedagogical features in my writing. After all, the research on memory and thinking tells us how to help students learn and remember. For example, in cognitive psychology, the self-reference effect informs us that the best way to learn something is to relate it to your own experience. I therefore include demonstrations that students can try in just a few minutes, using very little equipment. They can also become actively involved in the research, rather than remaining passive learners. We also know that people learn better if they read relatively small portions and review frequently, rather than trying to master an entire chapter at one time. Therefore, I divide each chapter into between two and five sections, with a brief review at the end of each section. I also avoid definitions or quotations in the margins of the textbook pages, because they distract students' attention from the flow of the chapter.

The general topic for this section—writing clearly—raises the interesting question of writing style. I suspect that no two psychology professors agree completely about the characteristics of an ideal writing style, and they probably cannot even identify the features that make the style of one writer more appealing than the style of another. In my own writing, I emphasize precision, straightforward sentence structure, and clear transitions between sentences. I dislike pretentious writing, just as I dislike pretentious teaching. However, I also resent patronizing writing; students can tell when an author is "talking down" to them. I should also mention that I love to write; I truly enjoy assimilating new information, creating useful examples, and explaining difficult concepts.

Good writers should surround themselves with good writing. In the last 3 years, I've returned to my favorite authors from high school—Jane Austen, George Eliot, and the Brontë sisters—as well as a new favorite, Anthony Trollope. Nothing in contemporary literature matches the wit, grace, subtlety, and insightful human observations of these nineteenth-century British novelists. My very favorite is probably Jane Austen's (1816/1961) *Emma*. When Austen describes the social consequences of a rude remark that Emma makes to her talkative older friend, Miss Bates, I find myself spellbound.

When revising a book, I update and revise every topic. However, I also review every paragraph to make certain that each sentence is appropriately clear, that any examples are well chosen, and that the organization is strong. The goal of writing clearly is absolutely essential in an introductory textbook.

Conveying the Content of Psychology

Obviously, another crucial goal for an introductory psychology textbook is to convey the most important information about our discipline. Most students entering the introductory course know far less about human memory than they know about trigonometry. Organizations such as Teaching of Psychology in the Secondary Schools encourage high school teachers to emphasize the natural science side of psychology. However, my sense is that most courses still focus on personal adjustment and "pop psych" approaches. We therefore need to help students understand why topics such as the cerebral cortex, the perception of movement, working memory, and decision making are interesting in their own right. We also need to emphasize that more complex social interactions depend on these more basic processes.

Unfortunately, part of the task of an introductory psychology author is to help students unlearn much of the misinformation they acquired about psychology during high school. For example, I was often dismayed to read the health textbook that my daughters used in their junior year of high school. Freudian theory was presented as documented fact, rather than a century-old collection of hypotheses. Students also enter our classes believing that concepts such as "midlife crisis" apply to all humans. The popular press also leads them to believe that hypnosis is a magical tool that unlocks buried memories.

One central concept that I try to convey in my approach is that psychological processes are complicated and subtle, rather than being governed by the simple, straightforward forces described by the media. Thus, the right hemisphere and the left hemisphere may process somewhat different kinds of information, but the differences are not as dramatic as most students initially believe. Furthermore, men may be more aggressive than women in some areas, but in other areas the gender differences are minimal. Again, our textbooks must not only teach new information; they must also correct misinformation.

Perhaps the most difficult task of any author is to decide which topics must be included in the book. This task becomes especially overwhelming when writing a revision. Authors must include hundreds of recently published articles and books, reporting the latest research developments. The reviewers who provide suggestions for revisions usually specify that we must not only update the coverage of previous topics, but we should also include many additional topics in the new edition. Furthermore, no topic from the previous edition should be dropped or shortened. However, the entire new edition should be about 20 pages shorter than the previous one—clearly a mathematical impossibility!

When deciding what to include (either in a first edition or a revision), I am guided by the goals I have for teaching the relevant course, such as my four goals for introductory psychology. Some of the topics I tend to exclude are those of only historical interest (such as phrenology), those on the periphery of psychology (such as parapsychology), and those that seem more relevant to disciplines other than psychology (such as the biochemistry of neuronal transmission). Reviewers usually provide useful information, but I am sometimes astonished to read some of the topics that they feel are essential for an introductory textbook. For example, one reviewer said that he could not imagine adopting a book that lacked substantial treatment of Vygotsky's theories in the child development chapter.

This complaint about course content raises another issue. If a professor teaches introductory psychology and discovers that a particular topic is missing from the textbook, couldn't he or she simply choose to lecture on this topic during class? Perhaps some professors devote their entire class periods to reviewing the material in the textbook. However, I suspect that most of us prefer to develop lectures and classroom exercises that complement the textbook, rather than duplicating it. Naturally, I can understand why professors might reject a particular book because it is too easy or because its approach is too applied or too cognitive in its orientation. I can also understand why other professors might reject a book that does not emphasize current research or that shortchanges multicultural issues. However, if a professor rejects a book because it neglects several idiosyncratic topics, I would question whether the professor has sincerely considered the difficulty of covering all the topics of psychology within a 700-page limit.

Another content issue that introductory psychology authors must address is the trade-off between breadth versus depth. Obviously, I wish I could write in depth about all relevant topics. This wish is especially intense for the chapters that represent topics on which I have written a textbook. How can sensation and perception be condensed into one 40-page chapter? The compromise I adopt is to leave out selected topics, rather than to try to be encyclopedic. For example, in the sensation and perception chapter of my introductory book, I do not discuss the vestibular and kinesthetic senses (even though they form a significant chunk of my *Sensation and Perception* textbook). To add some depth, I also cover one selected topic in each chapter in detail. For example, in the second edition of my introductory textbook, I chose illusory contours for the in-depth section. These in-depth sections emphasize research, and they often explore a particular research issue. For instance, the in-depth section of the learning chapter examines how three different research methods can be used to explore the effects of television violence on children; the advantages and disadvantages of each research method are also discussed.

Part of my purpose in conveying the content of psychology is to present students with information that may lead them to think about their values. For example, the chapter on child development contains some grim material on the welfare of children in North America during the 1990s. I would guess that students do not learn much about this topic in high school. One of my daughters brought home her high school social studies textbook, which prominently featured an American eagle on the cover. The entire emphasis of this textbook was on our wonderfully benevolent form of government, which defends democracy and righteousness throughout the world. "We're number one!" was the clear message. I hope that my readers will consider the textbook's information on the incidence of poverty and homelessness and question whether all is right with our nation. I also hope that they examine our government's treatment of Japanese Americans during World War II, a subject covered in the social psychology chapters. Most students do not learn in high school that our government can make mistakes.

As textbook authors, however, we must remain honest about the research. For example, I feel quite passionate about the issue of media violence. (In fact, our local peace group distributed literature at a toy store in Geneseo, New York, urging holiday shoppers to consider how violent toys and television can influence their children.) However, the discussion of media violence in my book points out that the correlation between media exposure and violent behavior is moderate, rather than strong. As a responsible psychologist, I cannot misrepresent the research.

Encouraging Critical Thinking

My doctorate degree is in experimental psychology, and my first textbook was *Human Experimental Psychology*. I have always enjoyed teaching about research design in my courses, because these discussions encourage students to think critically about the way research is conducted, and not simply the products of this research.

Because these research-design issues are so critical, I really believe that this topic deserves a separate chapter in an introductory psychology textbook. Students need to learn about the advantages and disadvantages of each research method. They need many examples of the correlational method, for instance, and they need to appreciate why correlations may not involve causal relationships. They should learn to be skeptical about research that lacks an appropriate control group or research that involves biased samples. They must also learn to differentiate between statistical and practical significance. A complete chapter on methodology at the beginning of an introductory psychology textbook encourages an attitude of healthy skepticism.

Students need to retain this critical attitude toward research throughout the entire course. Therefore, I raise methodological concerns wherever appropriate. For example, when discussing the visual agnosia research in the biological chapter, I ask students to consider whether confounding variables could explain some puzzling results. In the chapter on child development, we grapple with the difficulty of measuring the dependent variable in assessing infant perception. In a later chapter, we examine why placebo conditions are essential in conducting research on therapy for psychological disorders. The third edition of my textbook will also include six to eight active learning exercises in critical thinking for each chapter.

Critical thinking skills are especially important because students need to develop the ability to analyze the reports of psychological research that they encounter in the popular media—not only as college students but also after they leave academia. They need to know how to critique these summaries and how to determine what other attributes of the study they need to know before judging the research to be appropriately conducted. They should also be able to evaluate advertisers' claims. My research methods chapter therefore includes an extended example concerning advertisers' false claims about the value of subliminal tapes; this "research" did not include a control group that heard no subliminal message. Much of the information about the content of psychological research may disappear from the memories of our student readers, despite our best efforts to make the material especially memorable. However, their critical thinking skills should persist long after graduation if we emphasize research methods and encourage thoughtful analysis throughout a textbook.

Applying Psychology in Everyday Life

An introductory psychology textbook should also help students address some of the important problems that arise in their daily lives. I recently delivered the new-student convocation at the State University of New York (SUNY), Geneseo, and I titled my presentation, "Six Tips From Psychology to Make You Healthy, Happy, and Wise." These six hints are all issues that are emphasized in my own approach, and they represent some of the most important applications of our discipline. The first and most general hint is to overcome mindlessness (e.g., in problem solving). We need to think of new, more effective ways of generating solutions, rather than mindlessly repeating our customary habits. A second hint involves avoiding magical thinking, an issue that is addressed in such areas as alcohol abuse, sexual activity, and AIDS. A third hint is to overcome stereotypes, a topic I address in more detail in the next section of this chapter.

Tip number four is to try to resolve conflicts before they grow too large. Conflict resolution is discussed in some detail in chapter 18 of my book. The fifth tip emphasizes being positive in your interactions with other people. In the learning chapter, I stress the value of positive reinforcement, and in chapters 11 and 17, I discuss how the fundamental attribution error may make us unduly skeptical about the motivations for a friend's behavior. My final hint addressed why metacognitive skills are essential for developing appropriate study habits. Students do not learn how to think about their learning process when they are in high school, and introductory textbooks can encourage more mindful study habits.

As authors of introductory psychology textbooks, we must "give psychology away" and point out that psychologists can offer some practical advice that is backed by research evidence. I am not at all embarrassed to have a substantial applied focus in my approach; otherwise, students would rightfully question the ecological validity of psychology research. Furthermore, if students can apply a psychological principle to their own lives, the self-reference effect will operate to make the principle more meaningful and more memorable.

Addressing Diversity in Introductory Psychology

My own early experiences with diversity are probably similar to those of the other contributors to this volume. Throughout my years at both Stanford and Michigan, all of my psychology professors were men, except for Eleanor Maccoby. Furthermore, this lack of diversity did not strike me as strange until the early 1970s, when I decided to begin teaching a course in psychology of women. Obviously, a focus on gender is now an important component in both my introductory psychology classroom and in my textbook.

All of my professors in college and graduate school were also White. However, my first academic mentor was my high school biology teacher, Harry K. Wong, a man who was clearly proud of his Chinese American heritage. My own college, SUNY Geneseo, is located in the heart of upstate New York farmlands. Until recently, almost all of our students were White. At present, 15%–20% of our students are people of color. Although our college does not represent the heterogeneity of the U.S. population, I value the modest diversity of perspectives we now have in our classrooms. For example, an African American woman can comment on how distressed she is to see fashion catalogs in which the only Black women have pale tan skin and straightened hair. A student from El Salvador can talk about his difficulties in learning idiomatic English.

A Chinese man in my psychology of women class can talk about how his great grandmother had bound feet and could barely walk. Naturally, this diversity sometimes creates some unusual dilemmas. For example, last year a student from Nigeria came in to ask about a puzzling issue in my introductory psychology textbook. I had referred to an event as resembling something out of a soap opera—and he came in to ask me to explain what a soap opera was.

To acquire a broader background in other cultures, I have worked with the Hispanic student group on campus. This year, the Korean American student group asked me to be their adviser after the only professor with a Korean heritage moved back to Korea.

I have also acquired a better perspective on people with a Latin American background through my family's ongoing connection with Nicaragua. In 1990, I visited Rochester's sister city of El Sauce, Nicaragua, together with my husband Arnie (a pediatrician) and my eldest daughter, Beth, who has always been interested in early childhood education. Together, we decided that our family would create a Head Start type program for 30 malnourished preschoolers in El Sauce. On a subsequent visit, I was very impressed with the enthusiasm and generosity of these young children. Unlike American children from wealthy families, they played happily with each other—without excluding any child. They shared the toys equitably and did not whine or demand too much of the teacher's attention. This experience helped me appreciate that the spoiled American child is far from normative in the context of the world's children.

I have been fortunate to acquire other multicultural perspectives from my daughters (an exciting role reversal in which the children can teach their parents). Beth is currently teaching kindergarten in the Boston schools. Her two classes, totaling about 50 students each year, typically have only 2 or 3 White children. The majority of her children are African American, but a large number are also from Puerto Rico and various other Caribbean islands, Latin America, and Cape Verde (a Portuguese-speaking island off the coast of Africa). It's wonderful to hear her stories about these children—about the 4-year-old girl who acts as a translator for a classmate who speaks only Spanish or the excitement of a child who discovers that his Spanish-speaking classmate can understand some of his Portuguese words. Beth's stories about the caring Black mothers and their meticulously dressed children certainly defy the media images of inner-city women on welfare. However, she also tells us stories about child abuse and neglect, about children witnessing domestic violence, and about children whose uncles have been killed on the streets.

My daughter Sally has helped us understand more about Latin Americans because she has lived in Mexico, Nicaragua, and Brazil. As a student at Stanford she lived for 2 years at Casa Zapata, the university's Latin American theme dorm. During her junior year, she was the dorm's theme associate and organized a course on Chicana women. We appreciated her insights about gender in Hispanic culture, about creating a spirit of "la familia" in the dorm to encourage interdependence, and about Chicano students whose parents did not encourage them to master Spanish. Sally now lives in rural Nicaragua near the Honduran border, where she works as a community organizer. Her stories continue to inform my teaching and my writing, reminding me to enlarge my point of view.

Another source of diversity that has been important to me is the issue of sexual orientation or preference. When I began teaching, I assumed that all of my academic colleagues were heterosexual until I joined a women's consciousness-raising group in the 1980s. Of the four women in that group, I was the only heterosexual person. I found myself in the interesting position of being in the minority in a group where being lesbian was normative. This valuable perspective encouraged me to discuss issues of sexual preference and orientation in both my psychology of women and introductory psychology classes. For a period of about 5 years, I served as the faculty advisor of the Lesbian, Gay, and Bisexual Support Group on campus, during an era when none of the gay male or lesbian professors on campus felt comfortable about making their status known by advising the group. Dozens of students have come into my office and shared with me their stories about the pain and joy of coming out, about the homophobia they experience from their classmates, and about the strength they feel through having a reasonably visible support group on campus.

These experiences have persuaded me of the central importance of diversity in writing about psychology. The textbooks I used as an undergraduate in the 1960s were modeled on the normative White male, and nothing seemed wrong with that model 30 years ago. Now, however, I can appreciate that this model excludes the experiences of the majority of our students.

The first edition of my introductory textbook, published in 1992, emphasized diversity at a time when only one or two other books paid substantial attention to issues such as gender, ethnicity, and sexual orientation. Although many reviewers welcomed my emphasis on these issues, several other reviewers responded with hostility. I can clearly recall the words of one individual, "She is clearly trying to pander to all the minority professors." (Of course, I wondered whether this reviewer was aware just how few people of color actually teach introductory psychology.) Several reviewers also complained that many of the photos and figures in the book showed people of color.

Obviously, I am delighted to see that issues of diversity are now more welcome in introductory psychology and that virtually every introductory textbook now provides at least some coverage of the topics. However, the coverage is often superficial, and discussion of diversity is often confined to the final chapter of the book. This "back of the bus" treatment does not seem appropriate. Furthermore, professors may tend to eliminate this chapter if time is limited, and therefore students may view diversity issues as trivial or optional. Therefore, my approach incorporates gender and ethnicity within every relevant topic.

I also question the way the information is presented in some books. For example, a section on gender may emphasize gender differences, such as Carol Gilligan's (1982) work on moral development. This discussion may ignore the subsequent research that demonstrates gender similarities. The coverage of gender and intelligence may emphasize how male students receive higher scores on the Scholastic Aptitude Test in Arithmetic, ignoring the research on female students receiving higher grades in math courses. Ethnicity issues may be limited to the section on ethnic differences in IQ test scores, with little information on how people of color are misrepresented in ethnic stereotypes. The topic of sexual orientation may be placed in the section on AIDS. This placement suggests that gay and lesbian relationships are purely sexual (rather than romantic), that lesbian women are at high risk for AIDS, and that heterosexuals cannot get AIDS.

For me, a primary issue in examining diversity is to reduce students' stereotypes about a variety of issues. They need to learn that many gender differences are minimal, that many ethnic stereotypes have little basis in fact, and that the children of lesbians are typically as well-adjusted as the children of heterosexuals. They need to learn that elderly people may experience some loss in perceptual and cognitive skills, but those losses are seldom substantial or universal. They need to learn that (contrary to the implications of their high school textbooks) enemy images are unrealistic and in fact harmful.

In summary, a primary objective in my approach is to try to capture the diversity found in North America and to try to reduce the misinformation conveyed by the media and by popular stereotypes. By good fortune, we are writing for students who have obtained a degree of maturity and cognitive complexity. As a result, they may be eager to question their previous beliefs and to make decisions for themselves.

Some Final Concerns

One consequence of living at the end of a millennium is that we are especially likely to wonder about the future course of our endeavors. What course will introductory psychology textbooks take in the twenty-first century? Three issues seem especially important.

First, how will we handle the increasing amount of information about psychology? The initial outline for the first edition of my introductory textbook did not include a separate chapter on health psychology; topics such as stress, smoking, and AIDS were briefly incorporated into other chapters. However, my editors persuaded me to include this additional chapter. I am happy that I concurred, because information in this chapter may literally save some students' lives and because the content of the chapter provides an excellent review of numerous concepts from earlier chapters. However, does another obligatory chapter await us in 10 years?

In the third edition of my textbook, which I am currently writing, I would like to address two diversity issues—social class and cross-cultural research—in more detail. However, discussion of these topics means that more standard psychology topics would be discarded. What traditional topics are we prepared to abbreviate or abandon? Can I shorten the section on classical conditioning? Will people complain if I eliminate the discussion of hypnosis? Could I possibly condense the overview of theories of emotion? As I write each of these questions, I can visualize readers of this volume shaking their heads in dismay. I do not believe that psychologists or psychology textbook editors could ever agree on a list of topics that could safely be abandoned.

A second concern is that the publishing industry is not healthy. The cost of producing textbooks is rising, and the population of college students has declined (temporarily, I hope). When I search through the exhibit displays at conventions, I am continually reminded about the decreasing number of publishing companies. With bleak financial prospects, publishers are not eager to take interesting risks. For example, I've often discussed alternate models for introductory textbooks with other psychologists. Some professors, for instance, like to begin their course with social psychology, a topic that immediately engages the interest of students. Topics such as research methods, biological psychology, and sensation and perception are introduced at a later stage. I do not favor this model. However, it has enough supporters that a daring publisher could probably find this project to be financially rewarding. Financial uncertainty breeds conformity, however, rather than risk taking.

A third and final concern is the role of new technologies in introductory psychology. Laser discs, CD-ROMs, and other new technologies can certainly transcend the limits of the printed page. The topic of biological motion can be instantly appreciated after watching a few seconds of a film clip on a CD-ROM. A demonstration of sensory memory can be conveyed much more effectively on a laser disc than in a low-tech classroom demonstration.

Will the CD-ROM actually replace the textbook? The format is certainly more flexible than the printed page. However, we have not yet considered how students learn from this new media form. How do they take notes, how do they prepare the material for later review, and how do they study for examinations? The CD-ROM may present material effectively, but it may not teach as effectively as a textbook.

Similarly, some colleges and universities may lose sight of teaching goals as they become enchanted with new classroom technologies. At a recent teaching conference, Virginia Andreoli-Mathie (1995) discussed how she uses some of these new technologies in her social psychology classes at James Madison University. A well-equipped classroom clearly offers some exciting options for appealing visual presentations. However, she emphasized that each class session requires many hours to prepare. Furthermore, her time is often occupied with pressing buttons and adjusting equipment, rather than in more personal interactions with her students. I can certainly appreciate the advantages of these visually captivating technologies for classrooms with enormous enrollments. Even the most engaging professor needs some visual assistance in a class of 600 students!

The enrollment in my own introductory psychology class is limited to 110 students. Even this class size is not ideal. Lively discussions are less likely than in my classes of 40 students. Moreover, I cannot learn all students' names, as I do in my smaller classes. However, I am convinced that real teaching takes place in these classrooms through human interactions—through lecturing, conversations, demonstrations, and active-learning techniques. Although I welcome new ways of presenting information effectively, I am certain that students still value having an instructor who presents carefully organized material, asks thought-provoking questions, assesses whether they seem to have grasped the important concepts, and seems to care about their well-being. At least in the late 1990s, no CD-ROM or laser disc can accomplish these more human teaching goals.

References

Andreoli-Mathie, V. (1993). Promoting active learning in psychology courses. In T. V. McGovern (Ed.), *Handbook for enhancing undergraduate education in psychology* (pp. 183–214). Washington, DC: American Psychological Association.

Andreoli-Mathie, V. (1995, October) *Teacher or technician? Teaching in the 21st century.* Paper presented at the Northeastern Conference for Teachers of Psychology, Ithaca, NY.

Austin, J. (1961). *Emma.* London: J. M. Dent. (Original work published 1816)

Gilligan, C. (1982). *In a different voice.* Cambridge, MA: Harvard University Press.

Matlin, M. W. (1979). *Human experimental psychology.* Monterey, CA: Brooks/Cole.

Matlin, M. W. (1995a, August). *Invited address: American Psychological Foundation Teaching in Psychology Award. Gardeners, midwives, bankers . . . and barracudas: Metaphors for college teaching.* Paper presented at the 103rd Annual Convention of the American Psychological Association, New York.

Matlin, M. W. (1995b). *Psychology* (2nd ed.). Fort Worth, TX: Harcourt Brace.

Matlin, M. W. (1996). *The psychology of women* (3rd ed.). Forth Worth, TX: Harcourt Brace.

Matlin, M. W. (in press). *Cognition* (4th ed.). Forth Worth, TX: Harcourt Brace.

Matlin, M. W., & Foley, H. J. (1997). *Sensation and perception* (4th ed.). Boston: Allyn & Bacon.

Nodine, B. F. (1994, August). *G. Stanley Hall lecture series. Students write to learn in psychology courses.* Paper presented at the 102nd Annual Convention of the American Psychological Association, Los Angeles.

Charles G. Morris

Still Giving Psychology Away After All These Years

6

Teachers are guided by the objectives they hope to achieve. The objectives are sometimes stated explicitly; perhaps more frequently they are unanalyzed and simply taken for granted.

WOLFLE et al., 1952, p. 1, emphasis added

 s a graduate student at the University of Illinois in the 1960s, I participated in a graduate seminar on the teaching of psychology taught by Frank Costin. One of our tasks during the semester was to develop a set of explicit goals for the introductory psychology course. For background, we were assigned a book written by Bill McKeachie and John Milholland (1961) that summarized a conference on undergraduate curricula held at the University of Michigan in the summer of 1960. In turn, that book referenced a summer conference on undergraduate instruction that had been held a decade earlier at Cornell (Wolfle et al., 1952). Both books reflected deep and careful thought about undergraduate education in psychology, and both profoundly influenced the introductory course I developed in response to the assignment. Remarkably, my goals and philosophy for the introductory course have changed little in the ensuing 30 years. Some might see this as a sign of sheer stubbornness on my part, but I prefer to interpret it as a sign not only of the lasting value of the principles discussed at those two early conferences but also as a result of my spending the last three decades in the same psychology department with Bill McKeachie and John Milholland, who have been quick to put me back on the right path when I have been tempted to stray. Here, then, are the guiding principles I use for teaching introductory psychology both in the classroom and in my textbooks (Morris, 1996a, 1996b).

Course Content

The beginning course should, as far as possible, meet the needs of diverse groups of students and should not be narrowly tailored to specific subgroups of students. The most basic issue facing an instructor of introductory psychology is whether to teach one course for all students or to tailor the course to the needs of specific subgroups of students. Both the Cornell and Michigan conferees agreed that the beginning course should not be narrowly tailored to particular groups of students, and I concur. As Wolfle et al. (1952) noted: "The most important course in the curriculum is the introductory course. It is the only contact many students have with psychology. It should therefore be appropriate to the largest number of students" (p. 13). Thus, the beginning course must serve equally well those students who will take only one course in psychology (for some of whom it is simply a required course), those students with a moderate interest in psychology who might perhaps "minor" in the field, and those students who are potential psychology majors and perhaps even future professionals. It must serve liberal arts students, education students, nursing students, engineers, and others as well. Moreover, it should at some point address the very diversity of the students themselves—gender, racial, ethnic, age, and cultural diversity all come immediately to mind.

Trying to be all things to all people in a single course is no small challenge—there is always the danger that one will end up being nothing to anybody. What, then, should we teach in an introductory course that must meet the needs of diverse groups of students?

The focus of the introductory course should be on the contribution psychology can make to a liberal education. The Cornell conference identified four global objectives for all undergraduate psychology courses:

> (1) Intellectual development and a liberal education; (2) a knowledge of psychology, its research findings, its major problems, its theoretical integrations, and its contributions; (3) personal growth and an increased ability to meet personal and social adjustment problems adequately; (4) desirable attitudes and habits of thought, such as the stimulation of intellectual curiosity, respect for others, and a feeling of social responsibility. (Wolfle et al., 1952, pp. 2–3)

It is unrealistic to expect to achieve all four objectives in just a single course, and so it is necessary to select one or two objectives that are most appropriate and realistic given the course and the student population being served. My choice, and that of the Cornell conferees, has been to focus on the contribution psychology can make to liberal education. That choice seems especially appropriate in the introductory course where there is such a breadth of content and such diversity of students and where previous exposure to course content is slim to nonexistent.

What exactly are these "liberal education objectives?" I believe (as did both the Cornell and Michigan conferees) that at the least they must include (a) providing students with knowledge about psychology (the basic problems of psychology, central facts and principles, psychology as a science, and the structure and functioning of science); (b) changing ways of thinking (systematic and unbiased observation, quantitative thinking, and an understanding of multiple causation); and (c) changing values and attitudes (knowledge as a value and attitudes of caution and responsibility regarding psychological matter). Each of these objectives is discussed in greater detail, because they go to the heart of the beginning course as I envision it.

KNOWLEDGE OR CONTENT?

The introductory course should provide a systematic overview of the science of behavior and mental processes. The introductory course should not focus on immediate practical concerns or appeal to students' preconceived ideas about the nature of psychology (Wolfle et al., 1952). Rather, it should address the persistent, basic problems of psychology (problems with roots in history and in contemporary society as well as problems or topics that are shared with other disciplines); it should provide a broad sampling of the central facts and principles of psychology; and it should describe psychology as a science (including an overview of the scientific method). As noted by participants at the Michigan conference:

> All beginning courses in psychology should attempt to demonstrate and gain acceptance for the proposition that human behavior is a suitable object of study by scientific methods and to communicate the content material of basic psychology that has been attained by scientific methods. (McKeachie & Milholland, 1961, p. 41)

As a corollary, students should be made aware that psychology is not simply common sense, that it has "something to tell them about human character and behavior that they do not know already by virtue of having been practicing 'psychologists' all their lives" (McKeachie & Milholland, 1961, p. 42).

What specifically should be included in such a systematic overview of the science of psychology?

1. The introductory course should emphasize basic, core facts and principles. In my own teaching, I concentrate on those central facts and principles that are widely (if not universally) accepted, that are important for any well-educated person to know, and that are necessary as preparation for advanced courses. If a particular topic does not meet at least two of these three criteria, then it will almost certainly not find a place in my course or in my texts. This is a highly selective approach to course content that will not meet with universal approval. Some of my colleagues, for example, teach a genuinely encyclopedic course, cramming as much material as possible between the covers of the semester. Perhaps they fear that their students will forget so much that they should fill them twice as full to begin with! An alternative strategy, and the one I prefer, is to stick to the core content and teach it in a way that it is less likely to be forgotten. The techniques I use to accomplish this end are described in greater detail later in this chapter.

   Some of my colleagues also subscribe to the belief that "when teaching the better students, the number of facts, principles, and theories covered in the course should be increased significantly." According to this logic, if a 600-page text is appropriate for most students, an 800-page text is likely to be even better for honors students or students at highly selective institutions. However, if the 600-page text effectively covers the basic, core facts and principles of psychology, what is the purpose of assigning another 200 pages? In contrast, I use the same brief textbook for all of my introductory courses—the large survey course, small honors courses, extension courses taught in the evening in nearby cities, the whole works. Instead of assigning a longer text and simply increasing the quantity of material with the better students, I use the opportunity to augment their learning experience in qualitatively different ways (such as the computer conferences and outside reading projects I describe later in this chapter).

   Some of my colleagues believe it is important to personalize their introductory courses and textbooks, in effect teaching "Introduction to Psychology and Me," in which their personal attitudes, values, and agendas become inextricably mixed with the core content of psychology. In contrast, I make a concerted effort not to intrude on the content of psychology. I believe that the discipline and agendas of psychology should be the focus and center of the students' attention, not me and my personal experiences or values or attitudes. To the extent that I succeed in following this principle, my students and readers should come away with a greater awareness of the agendas that are widely shared by psychologists and yet find it difficult or impossible to determine my personal position on other controversial issues. I return to this issue shortly, in the Values and Attitudes section.

2. The introductory course should include some of the exciting new developments in the field that will likely have lasting value. Current research and theory should have a place in the introductory course. As instructors, we certainly should attempt to cover as best we can those new developments that appear to be both significant and of lasting value. This not only assures that our course is contemporary but also provides our students with a sense of the dynamic nature of the field. However, we do our students a grave disservice if, in an artificial attempt to look "current" or to create a sense of "freshness," we teach material that will not stand the test of time. Unfortunately, the task of identifying genuinely important new work is especially difficult for those of us who teach the introductory course because much of the time we are operating out of our own area of special expertise. How, then, is an introductory teacher or textbook author to resolve the dilemma of remaining current without heeding every siren call and being distracted by fads or "flash in the pan" research? One excellent approach is to rely on colleagues who are experts to provide advice on what new developments in their field can reasonably be included in the beginning course. In the late 1970s, the American Psychological Association's (APA) Committee on Undergraduate Education under my chairmanship proposed the creation of the G. Stanley Hall lecture series at the APA convention specifically as a forum in which content experts could tell introductory instructors what is new and important in their respective subfields; that lecture series continues to serve well its original purpose. In addition, publications such as *Current Directions in Psychological Science, American Psychologist,* the *Annual Review of Psychology,* and the recently released four-volume *Encyclopedia of Human Behavior* (Ramachandran, 1994) are

excellent sources of information about important trends and new developments across the entire range of the field.

3. The introductory course should provide students with a sense of the historical development of the field and the way in which our current understandings developed. Although it is important to cover contemporary developments in the field as described above, I think it is an error to teach only "psychology today" as if there was no yesterday. Like the Cornell and Michigan conferees, I believe that it is important for students to gain at least some understanding of how psychology developed even though some of the ideas are no longer generally considered valid.

4. The introductory course should teach psychology as a science. Decades ago, the Michigan conferees "held firmly to the point of view that in the beginning course, no less than in the remainder of the curriculum, the essential character of psychology as a science should be maintained" (McKeachie & Milholland, 1961, p. 52). That goal is as important today as it was in 1960. The beginning course should systematically set out to attack the popular image of psychology as simply an applied field and replace that image with an understanding that psychology is, in fact, an attempt to gain insight into behavior through science. The course should demonstrate how psychology uses the scientific method to address questions and how knowledge in psychology accumulates across many studies and over time. Commonsense views of behavior should be contrasted with the (often surprising) results of systematic research on the same topics. Students should come to see exactly how empirical research has caused psychologists to rethink their views on numerous topics, just as it should cause the students themselves to rethink some of their own views.

I have devoted a great deal of space to a discussion of the "knowledge or content" component of the introductory course because inevitably the greatest emphasis in most introductory courses and texts is put on knowledge and content. The Cornell conferees anticipated this when they pointed out that

> values, attitudes, and habits of thought are legitimate goals to seek, but they are, nevertheless, relatively personal or private attributes of the student. Consequently, it is probably desirable to avoid direct frontal efforts to modify student's habits and attitudes. . . . [Moreover,] if the teacher does not believe that the content of what he is teaching is important, he had better not

teach; and the students had better not listen. (Wolfle et al., 1952, p. 10)

Thus, although the following objectives are important to an introductory course in psychology, they are likely to be "second and third among equals" when it comes to allocating time in most introductory courses and space in most introductory texts, my own included.

HABITS OF THOUGHT

The introductory course should encourage rigorous habits of thought. The introductory psychology course should certainly make a difference in the way students think about and perceive psychological information. Moreover, students who take a beginning course in psychology should emerge as more sophisticated observers of behavior, understanding the potential pitfalls in observing and interpreting spontaneous behavior in an uncontrolled setting. They should also develop some skill in quantitative thinking (e.g., the nature of scales, the need for precise measurement, the basic logic of statistical inference, and the logic of sampling). They should develop their capacity to think critically: to evaluate evidence carefully, to be aware of illogical thinking, to recognize overgeneralizations, and to distinguish correlation from causation. They should also develop a greater appreciation for the fact that most behavior has multiple causes, and as a result, they should be less likely to arrive at oversimplified explanations for complex behaviors. They should exercise greater caution in reasoning about behavior, showing greater awareness of assumptions, biases, limitations, and probabilities that set limits on what they know. They also should become more able to judge their own behavior objectively. In short, they should come to think more like scientists.

VALUES AND ATTITUDES

The introductory course should encourage attitudes and values that are consistent with our understanding of psychological processes. Without presuming to identify values and attitudes that everyone would endorse, I think there would be general agreement that a beginning course in psychology might legitimately foster or encourage "attitudes of intellectual curiosity, of respect for others, and of social responsibility" (Wolfle et al., 1952, p. 3). It is not inappropriate to encourage students to value knowledge and thinking and learning for their own sake, to understand that "worth" is not always measured by "payoff." It is also appropriate to attempt to awaken and develop a genuine interest in psychology, to create an understanding of and respect for psychology and psychologists, and to increase support for scientific and scholarly research in psychology as well as prevention of mental illness and treatment of the mentally ill. Moreover, it is reasonable for the introductory course to attempt to develop tolerance toward the mentally ill and to foster a greater appreciation of human diversity (McKeachie & Milholland, 1961).

Teaching Techniques

It is one thing to decide the objectives and the proper content for a course, but it is quite another to achieve the desired results. That's the stuff of "teaching tactics." The following tactics or techniques have served me well in translating objectives into reality in the introductory course.

USE OF A TEXTBOOK

Given my earlier emphasis on presenting a systematic overview of psychology, it should come as no surprise that I rely heavily on a textbook. Therein lies a story: In the mid- to late-1960s, when I first started teaching introductory psychology, I was simply unable to find a textbook that met all my needs. There were several very good, high-level texts available, but they were far too encyclopedic and not very stimulating to read. There were also numerous "pop psychology" texts that appeared to be driven primarily by student interests, catchy topics, relevance, and transparent gimmicks; these texts were often interesting and fun to read but at the cost of solid content.

Caught as I was between "too much" and "too little," I implored textbook publishers to produce a solid, respectable, comprehensive yet relatively brief introductory textbook that would do justice to the core principles and findings of psychology and that would also be readable and interesting to students without resorting to gimmicks. Not surprisingly, the typical reply was "There is no such thing—why don't you write one yourself?" I set out to do just that with *Psychology: An Introduction,* which is now in its ninth edition (Morris, 1996a). Over the years, its format has been widely emulated, so the instructor who shares my philosophy of teaching now has a choice among several excellent textbooks. I wish I had been as fortunate 30 years ago.

In any event, the textbook is the core of my introductory course, and I make it clear to students that I expect them truly to master the content of the text. To assist them in that endeavor, I use several teaching techniques.

PRESENTATION OF MATERIAL

In my classroom as well as my texts, I make it a habit to start where students are, and then to draw them slowly into the content I want to get across. In the process I attempt to show them gradually how a different approach makes more sense of the facts. Sometimes I use a Platonic dialogue to show that common sense or obvious answers do not hold up under close scrutiny. At other times I attempt to contrast research data and student preconceptions. In each case, the goal is to build from the concrete and specific to more general principles, from simplicity to greater complexity, in much the way that Piagetian accommodation represents a change in thinking in response to experience.

Most often, however, I use a common example, a case study, or a demonstration that taps into student interests and, at the same time, provides a base on which to build more sophisticated understanding. For example, in class I describe at some length the "son of Sam" serial murder case to provide a base from which we can then consider schizophrenia and the difference between the legal concepts of competence and insanity on the one hand and the concept of mental illness on the other. I also put on a lengthy slide show of various visual illusions to show dramatically that illusions arise at different levels in the visual system and to demonstrate powerfully the extent to which perception is an active, creative process that goes far beyond what students normally realize. I have students try to memorize various kinds of information to drive home the notion that memory is organized, that retrieval cues are critical to retrieval from long-term memory, that there is often a serial position effect, and that proactive and retroactive interference is important to understanding why we remember some things and forget others.

I take the same approach in my writing. For example, the chapter-opening pieces in my texts are not simply window dressing; rather, they set the stage for the discussion that follows, often raising in simple terms key points that are addressed in the chapter. In the motivation chapter I use a discussion of weight loss as a way to reemphasize what psychology has discovered about the determinants of hunger and eating behavior. In the cognition chapter, I include a number of problems for the reader to solve, each of which demonstrates an important principle that is discussed in greater detail in the text. The intelligence chapter starts with some questions drawn from various intelligence tests, not only to pique the readers' interest in the ensuing discussion of the nature of intelligence but to build on their experience with such tests and to lay the foundation specifically for a discussion of test reliability and validity later in the chapter. In each case, the ultimate goal is to demonstrate how psychology can add to what students already know about human behavior and to show them how the scientific method complements and differs from the approach they use in their own lives.

This tactic of "starting where the students are" is consistent with what is known of elaborative rehearsal and human memory: Systematically linking new material to what the students already know embeds the new material in long-term memory with lots of readily available retrieval cues. Recognition of the value of this technique predates contemporary cognitive theory. Decades ago, the Cornell conferees noted the following:

> Teachers will profit from learning what their students expect, what they already know about psychology, and what they feel their needs to be. This knowledge may not change the teacher's views as to what is important in his field, but it will enable him to start where his students are and to carry them as far as possible toward attainment of curricular objectives. (Wolfle et al., 1952, p. 1)

There are two caveats worth mentioning here: First, student interests should be used as a vehicle for teaching the core principles of psychology; they should not become ends in themselves. As the Michigan conferees noted, "if we fail to build from the concrete and specific to more general principles, we have failed to teach adequately" (McKeachie & Milholland, 1961, p. 28). Second, "good instruction must also stimulate and extend interests beyond matters on which students show spontaneous curiosity" (Wolfle et al., 1952, p. 14). As I noted earlier in this chapter, in part our task as instructors is to awaken and develop a genuine interest in psychology, to generate new interests where they do not necessarily exist, and in this way to affect student attitudes and values.

In addition to building on students' existing interests and knowledge, I also work hard to make the presentation of material interesting and engaging. As an undergraduate, I was always frustrated by professors who seemed to think that the more important something was, the less understandable they should make it to their students. It seemed to me that there was an unwritten rule that said "This concept is so important, it cannot possibly be explained clearly and simply. In fact if you understand what I am saying, then it must not be anything very important." Throughout my teaching career, I have become firmly convinced that even the most complex material in introductory psychology can be explained clearly and understandably (though at times I tear my hair seeking that level of clarity). One simple technique has served me well for decades: I imagine that I am presenting the topic in an after-lunch speech to a community service group or that I am explaining it to a relative or friend who has no background whatsoever in psychology. By keeping those audiences very much in mind while I am preparing lectures or writing manuscripts, I find it much easier to avoid the opaque, soporific style of presentation that otherwise seems to come so naturally to those of us ensconced in the halls of academe.

STUDY OBJECTIVES

Another knowledge-oriented technique that I have found extremely useful is to provide my students with detailed study objectives for each chapter of the textbook. These study objectives describe exactly what I mean when I refer to *mastery* of the textbook content. For example, for the section of the first chapter that deals with the experimental method, my student study objectives are the following:

> Understand the key features of the experimental method and the advantages and disadvantages of this method. Be sure you can distinguish between independent and dependent variables and between experimental and control groups. Be able to explain why control groups are used in experiments.

In the section of the learning chapter on advanced concepts in operant conditioning, the study objectives are the following:

> Understand what is meant by "reinforcement" and be able to distinguish between positive reinforcement and negative reinforcement and between primary reinforcement and secondary reinforcement. Be able to describe the effect of delay of reinforcement and different schedules of reinforcement on operant conditioning and to recognize examples of various schedules of reinforcement. Understand and be able to recognize examples of extinction, spontaneous recovery, generalization, and discrimination in operant conditioning. Be able to describe the factors that influence the resistance of a response to extinction.

There are roughly a dozen study objectives of this sort for each chapter of the text and more than 150 for the course as a whole.

Colleagues who have seen the complete list of objectives often say that students cannot possibly be expected to learn all that material. In fact, my students typically do an excellent job of mastering the material and meeting the objectives, at least in part perhaps because I show them exactly how to do so. I distribute the study objectives at the start of the course. I then provide a brief lecture on the importance of elaborative rehearsal in human memory and tell them step-by-step exactly how to use the study objectives to rehearse the content of each chapter effectively: (1) Read the objectives before reading the corresponding chapter; (2) open the book and attempt to develop an answer to the first chapter objective; (3) close the book, rehearse the answer, and then check the book for accuracy; (4) proceed to the second study objective, and so on through the chapter; (5) at the end of the chapter, close the book and rehearse from memory all the study objectives for that chapter, highlighting for further study those that cause any difficulty; and (6) repeat Step 5 several times in the ensuing weeks, focusing especially on the highlighted (potentially troublesome) objectives. I also reinforce the importance of the study objectives in classroom discussions (e.g., by asking students chosen at random to answer one or another study objective). The test questions on my exams are also keyed to the study objectives, and I ensure that every study objective is represented at least once on each exam.

PRACTICE TEST QUESTIONS

Another knowledge-oriented technique that I have found useful is to provide students in advance with some of the questions from my own test item file. In the past, I provided students with half of my entire test item file (but without answers!) and assured them that half of the questions on each exam would come from these items. Students then typically worked together to determine the correct answer to each of the questions; and whereas I agreed to help them work their way through the more difficult questions on which they were unable to arrive at a consensus, I steadfastly refused simply to give them the correct answer to any question.

I now use a somewhat different version of this same technique. I assemble all of the test questions that I used a year or so ago, organize them by chapter and study objective, and make them available (with an answer key) as "diagnostic self-tests" for each chapter. I urge students to study the chapter using the study objectives, then to take the diagnostic self-test for that chapter and score themselves to see how well they have mastered the material and to determine where they need to do more studying. I devote some class time to helping them work through questions on which they simply do not understand the correct answer.

For instructors who are reluctant to reveal questions from their actual test item file, there are alternative sources of useful practice questions. The student study guide for most texts typically includes test questions, and many texts also provide end-of-chapter self-tests that can be used effectively. The key, of course, is to ensure that the practice questions correspond closely both to the study objectives and to the kinds of questions that will actually be on the exams.

I find that students score about 5%–10% higher on the test questions they have seen than the questions they have not. Thus, if students average 75% on the unseen questions, typically they will score

80%–85% on the questions they have seen in advance. In addition to better mastery of course content, a number of secondary benefits derive from this technique of providing practice test questions. Students who ask "Will we be expected to know_____on the exam?" can be referred to the practice test questions for an answer. Moreover, students seem to be considerably less anxious when they know that the exam will include a number of familiar questions. Finally, comparing student performance on the practice questions and the unfamiliar questions that appeared on the exam is often very helpful when trying to determine why the student might be having difficulty on the exams.

PARTICIPATION IN RESEARCH

Students are required to spend 5 hours during the semester serving as experiment participants, after which they receive both verbal and written feedback from the experimenter.[1] Traditionally, the department's Human Subjects committee has been almost rabid in its dedication to ensure that the experience of serving as an experiment participant has real educational value. In fact, during the time I chaired the committee, one of my colleagues came to my office and asked incredulously, "Do you mean that if my research has little or no educational value, I cannot use the department subject pool?" The only honest reply was simply "Yes, that's correct." I have discussed elsewhere the potential educational value of participating in a research study, the steps that we have taken at the University of Michigan to ensure that the subject pool experience is indeed of educational value, and the evidence obtained from many years of systematic student evaluations that in fact the experience does have considerable educational value (Morris, 1990).

OUTSIDE READING PROJECTS

Because I use a brief textbook that nonetheless covers the core content of psychology, the better students have time to engage in qualitatively different activities that enrich their learning experience. For example, I provide my students with an annotated bibliography of more than 300 popular books in psychology. Each student then constructs a personal reading project consisting of one or more books from the list. The students maintain reading journals that are submitted twice each semester for grading and feedback. Depending on the qual-

---

[1]Students are given the alternative of summarizing five empirical articles published in APA journals.

ity and quantity of outside reading, the reading project counts for 20%–50% of the course grade. The syllabus is explicit about what should be in the reading journal:

> In it you should record your thoughts about what you are reading. You will have to engage yourself actively in the readings—passive note taking or highlighting won't suffice; you'll need to grapple with the ideas that are being discussed, compare them to what others have written, match them to your own experiences, look for contradictions and inconsistencies and exceptions and limitations, challenge the authors, talk about and test out the ideas with friends and roommates and family, and in general be an active, thinking participant in an ongoing dialogue with the authors of the readings.

For those who are interested, the bibliography is available on-line on the World Wide Web at

http://www-personal.umich.edu/~tmorris/goodbook.html.

An ASCII copy of the bibliography can be downloaded using a Web browser from

http://www-personal.umich.edu/~tmorris/goodbook.bin.

COMPUTER CONFERENCING

One other teaching technique deserves mention not only because it has been very successful but also because it serves especially well the second and third liberal education goals mentioned earlier (changing ways of thinking and changing attitudes and values). I have collected nearly 150 stimulating, controversial, open-ended discussion topics that span the full range of the course content. I post those questions on a computer bulletin board, provide each student with a computer account, and require that they sign on at least three times a week to participate actively in the discussion of at least half the posted questions. These conferences have turned out to be stunningly successful: The last time I used this technique, the transcript of the on-line discussions for just one semester in a course of only 30 students came to 4,000 double-spaced pages—the equivalent of 300–400 term papers or 10 books the size of this one! The average student spent 60 hours on-line during the semester. At one point, in a desperate measure of self-defense, the students voted unanimously to shut down the conference completely for 2 weeks so they could attend to their other courses without worrying that they would miss something interesting in the on-line discussions!

Because students in a computer conference of this type can carefully examine the comments posted by others and think carefully about their own opinions before posting a response (and then return subsequently to follow up on their previous comments), the discussions typically are far deeper and more sophisticated than classroom discussions of the same topics. Fuzzy thinking, uncritical assumptions, and overgeneralizations are quickly identified as such by other participants; cautious, scientific thinking becomes noticeably more evident as the semester progresses. Moreover, many of the discussion topics are chosen because they touch on important attitudes and values; thus, students are forced to confront their own beliefs about such value-laden issues as involuntary commitment, the use of animals in psychological research, the effectiveness of corporal punishment, the significance of sexist and racist language, the effects of labeling people, and the effect of television on children. Finally, students who are reluctant to speak up in class rarely have the same problem on-line; in fact, many such students say that this is the first time they have ever felt free to share their opinions, and they enjoy the fact that others are listening to them and learning from them.

A modification of this conferencing technique is now incorporated in my texts. Every chapter has a section headed "On-line" in which I describe one of the discussion topics related to that chapter, pose some challenging questions, and then quote from the comments some of my former students have made on that topic. Readers are then invited to consider their own positions on the issue and to join other readers on-line (on America Online or the Internet) for a coast-to-coast discussion of that and other, similar, controversial issues.

Psychology for the Next Millennium

Though I am generally satisfied with the introductory course as I have described it, I cannot resist a closing comment that entertains a very different approach to teaching the beginning course in psychology. Imagine the chapters of the standard textbook as rows in a table; now imagine columns made up of interesting issues in psychology (such as sleep and dreaming, memory, anger and aggression, mental abilities, love, stress, attitudes and values, abnormal behavior, and individual differences). Wouldn't it be fun to teach a beginning psychology course organized around the columns rather than around the rows? One might spend a week or two discussing sleep and dreaming, in the course of which it would be possible to talk about insights provided from psychobiology, cognitive psychology, developmental psychology, personality, and so on. Similarly, a week or two devoted to anger and aggression could draw on research in psychobiology, learning, development, motivation and emotion, personality, abnormal psychology, and social psychology. Love and intimacy similarly could be examined from multiple perspectives. Over the course of the semester, students would eventually be exposed to much of the content of the standard introductory course, but it would be presented in contexts where it might be more likely to be seen as coherent, relevant, and meaningful. Students might leave such a course with a less encyclopedic grasp of the field of psychology but perhaps with more of an understanding of how psychology can provide valuable insight into issues that are of interest and importance to virtually everyone. Perhaps someone who reads this will be inspired to develop the materials for such a course and set us off down a very different path in our continuing effort to "give psychology away."

References

McKeachie, W. J., & Milholland, J. E. (1961). *Undergraduate curricula in psychology.* Chicago: Scott, Foresman.

Morris, C. G. (1990, August). *Improving the introductory psychology subject pool.* Poster session presented at the 98th Annual Convention of the American Psychological Association, Boston.

Morris, C. G. (1996a). *Psychology: An introduction* (9th ed.). Upper Saddle River, NJ: Prentice Hall.

Morris, C. G. (1996b). *Understanding psychology* (3rd ed.). Upper Saddle River, NJ: Prentice Hall.

Ramachandran, V. S. (Ed.). (1994). *Encyclopedia of human behavior* (Vols. 1–4). San Diego, CA: Academic Press.

Wolfle, D., Buxton, C. E., Cofer, C. N., Gustad, J. W., MacLeod, R. B., & McKeachie, W. J. (1952). *Improving undergraduate instruction in psychology.* New York: Macmillan.

David G. Myers

Professing Psychology With Passion 7

There are still two sorts of job. Of one sort, a [person] can truly say, "I am doing work which is worth doing. It would still be worth doing if nobody paid for it. But as I have no private means, and need to be fed and housed and clothed, I must be paid while I do it." The other kind of job is that in which people do work whose sole purpose is the earning of money; work which need not be, ought not to be, or would not be, done by anyone in the whole world unless it were paid.

> C. S. Lewis
> *The World's Last Night*

ow fortunate we who profess psychology are to have the first sort of job. To present our discipline to the next generation, to convey the power of its ideas, to help students think more critically and gain insight into the phenomena of their everyday lives, to sense the extraordinary wonders beneath seemingly ordinary processes—such aims make our work intrinsically worth doing. And such aims motivate my own efforts to follow George Miller's (1969) admonition to give psychology away.

Having spent nearly three decades at a liberal arts college, where my friends and colleagues include philosophers, sociologists, biologists, and literary scholars, I am somewhat less concerned than others might be with teaching signal-

---

Quotations from literary and historical sources, which I have collected over the years, have been included with attribution but without full source citations.

detection theory's ROC curves and somewhat more concerned with teaching big ideas that cast psychology in the tradition of the liberal arts. By the teaching of literature, philosophy, natural science—and psychology—liberal education seeks to expand our thinking and awareness. Once one is aware of psychology's hard-wrought ideas about how body and mind connect, how a child's mind grows, how the mind constructs perceptions, memories, and beliefs, or how folks across the world differ and are alike, one's mind may never again be quite the same. "Once expanded to the dimensions of a larger idea," noted Oliver Wendell Holmes, the mind "never returns to its original size." My aim, whether teaching or writing (i.e., teaching to a wider classroom), is to present a psychology that is at once solidly scientific and warmly human, factually rigorous and intellectually provocative. Because I teach liberal arts students whose majors will usually not be psychology, I aim to represent psychology's breadth with a special focus on humanly significant issues.

Working in a student-centered institution, and as a parent of college-age children, my audience is primarily students, not colleagues. I am teaching my discipline to people who are often in the process of defining their goals, identities, values, and attitudes. Chaim Potok recalls being urged by his mother to forgo writing: "Be a brain surgeon. You'll keep a lot of people from dying; you'll make a lot more money." Potok's response: "Mama, I don't want to keep people from dying; I want to show them how to live" (quoted by Peterson, 1992, p. 47).

Many psychology teachers and writers are driven not only by a love for giving psychology away but also by wanting to help students live better lives—wiser, more fulfilling, more compassionate lives. In this we are like teachers and writers in other fields. "Why do we write?" asks theologian Robert McAfee Brown. "I submit that beyond all rewards . . . *we write because we want to change things*. We write because we have this [conviction that we] can make a difference. The 'difference' may be a new perception of beauty, a new insight into self-understanding, a new experience of joy, or a decision to join the revolution." Elie Wiesel agrees: "Words can sometimes, in moments of grace, attain the quality of deeds" (quotes from Marty, 1988, p. 2).

Values, Teaching, and Texts

In suggesting that our agenda as teachers and text writers goes beyond teaching signal-detection principles, I admit that certain values fuel and guide my efforts. Although my orientation is empiricist rather than postmodern subjectivist, postmodernists are surely justified in reminding us that values inevitably guide our research and reporting. Ironically, rigorous research helps make the point. Experiments on "confirmation bias," "belief perseverance," "mental set," and the "overconfidence phenomenon" demonstrate that belief often guides perception. Moreover, whether hidden or explicit, our values leak through our choice of teaching topics, our examples and emphases, and our labeling of phenomena.

Consider the values hidden in our terminology: Should we call sexually restrained people *erotophobic* or *sexually conservative*? Should we label those who say nice things about themselves on personality tests as "high self-esteem" or "defensive"? Should we congratulate socially responsive people for their social sensitivity or disparage them for their tractable conformity? (Reflecting our culture's individualistic values, American psychology's terminology places a premium on maximizing the independent self, as opposed to the interdependent self valued in Asian cultures.) Without throwing scientific rigor out with the bath water, psychology's value ladenness is something we can reveal in our teaching.

Thus, neither psychological science nor our reporting of it is dispassionate. Our preconceived ideas and values—our schemas—guide our theory development, our interpretations, our choice of topics, and our language. In our quest for truth, we follow our hunches, our biases, our voices within.

When writing, therefore, text authors cannot leave their values at home. In deciding *what* to report and *how* to report it, our own sympathies subtly steer us one way or another. Psychology texts are a pleasure to write precisely because they marry not only science with journalism, but facts with values. Although authors must be wary of using their texts as platforms for promoting any ideology, their values will leak through.

My values leak through my effort to cultivate a sense of wonder, an attitude that respects the human creature and regards it with awe. My values also leak through my decisions to give significant attention to topics such as cultural diversity, gender and racial prejudice, altruism, violence, individualism, peacemaking, pride, evil, and sex and human values. If I evaded these topics I would still be making value-laden decisions. *The choices authors and teachers face often preclude absolute neutrality.*

We need not apologize for having deeply held convictions and values, because our values are what motivates and directs our efforts. What has driven me to keep teaching and writing is a passion for communicating things more important than the correct definition of negative reinforcement. What greater life mission could one hope for than to do one's part to restrain intuition with critical thinking, judgmentalism with compassion, and illusion with understanding?

As I explained to one of my editors last year (after being chastised for providing information on the corroding well-being of children and its links to rising individualism and the decline of father care), I whole-heartedly agree that lecterns are not pulpits and textbooks are not op-ed columns. There is a place for some checks on the abuse of academic power by irresponsible ideologues. However,

> I can't give you, because no author can give you, a value-free psychology text. Often, I suspect, you won't notice my embedded values (when they agree with yours and with those of academia). But they'll be there. And it is because they are inevitably there in this value-laden field that I find a continuing sense of mission in my work for you.... Even if I aggravate you at times and need reigning in, I don't think you'd want to eviscerate the passions that drive me to write.

Reporting research findings pertinent to controversial issues can make editors wince (when some potential adopters wince). At such points, one faces a text author's greatest challenge: discerning how to be true to one's discipline and oneself, without being stubbornly closed to editorial and reviewer guidance. Where is the fine line between listening sensitively to editors' advice and capitulating to publisher censorship, between being open to the opinions of one's teaching colleagues and lusting for their adoptions? The humanly significant issues that psychology addresses do occasionally lead teachers—and text writers—into hot water. So be it, I recently explained to my publisher:

> My overarching aim is to discern and effectively communicate truth. In doing that, I also want to have the courage to let the chips fall where they may, even if data on sexual orientation make conservatives uncomfortable, even if data on viewing sexual violence make liberals uncomfortable, even if the data from tests of parapsychology make New Age spiritualists uncomfortable. In these and other areas, my aim is not to make the news, but to report it as fairly and honestly as I can ... and to promote critical thinking. I suppose I could self-censor research findings on controversial topics. But if reporting research stimulates a little debate, and if the writing has a personal voice, isn't that desirable?

Teaching Objectives

If these are the overarching motivations and values that energize my teaching and writing, what are the pedagogical objectives and tactics?

1. *To exemplify the process of inquiry*. I strive to show students not just the outcome of research, but how the research process

works. I aim to excite students' curiosity. I want them not only to acquire knowledge, but to love learning. I therefore invite students to imagine themselves as participants in classic experiments and often introduce research stories as mysteries that progressively unravel as one clue after another is put into place.

2. *To teach critical thinking.* By presenting research as intellectual detective work, I aim to exemplify an inquiring, analytical mind-set. Whether students are studying development, cognition, or statistics, I want to involve them in critical reasoning (after giving them the necessary tools) and to display its rewards. Thus I begin my course and text by emphasizing how psychological science is an antidote to the pitfalls of unaided intuition. Throughout the course, students then see how an empirical approach can help us evaluate competing ideas and claims for highly publicized phenomena—ranging from subliminal persuasion, ESP, and facilitated communication to astrology, basketball streak shooting, and repressed and recovered memories. If the tabloids were to cover my course, I would welcome the headline, "Think Smarter With Psychological Science!"

3. *To put facts in the service of concepts.* My intention has been not to fill students' intellectual file drawers with facts, but to reveal psychology's major concepts—to teach students how to think and to offer psychological ideas worth thinking about. Starting with a first-session demonstration of the "hindsight bias" (aka the I-knew-it-all-along phenomenon), I place emphasis on those concepts I hope students will carry with them long after they complete the course.

4. *To integrate principles and applications.* Throughout the course, I apply the findings of basic research to life (by means of anecdotes, case histories, and the posing of hypothetical situations), believing that students' lives matter more to them than knowing psychology, yet also believing that their own lives can hook their interest in psychology. Anecdotes, though often misleading as data, can memorably illuminate important principles. Where psychology can illuminate pressing human issues—be they racism and sexism, health and happiness, or violence and war—I do not hesitate to shine its light.

5. *To enhance comprehension by providing continuity.* I try to weave into many class sessions and text chapters a significant issue or theme that links subtopics, forming a thread that ties things together. The class session on "illusory thinking" raises the issue of human rationality and irrationality. The session on psychological disorders conveys empathy for and under-

standing of troubled lives. By teaching and writing solo, I also aim to weave, throughout the course, threads such as nature–nurture interaction and cultural diversity. The uniformity of a work, according to Edward Gibbon, denotes the hand of a single artist. Perhaps the same could be said of a class taught by a single teacher who comes to know and to be known by each student.

6. *To convey respect for human unity and diversity.* Time and again, I offer students evidence for our human kinship—our shared biological heritage, our common mechanisms of seeing and learning, hungering and feeling, loving and hating. They also learn the dimensions of our diversity—our individual diversity in development and aptitudes, temperament and personality, and disorder and health and our cultural diversity in attitudes and expressive styles, child rearing and care for the elderly, and life priorities. Knowing that my student audience is international, and believing that North American students, too, would benefit from a greater world consciousness, I work to present a more world-based psychology, inclusive of global research findings, demographic information, and cultural examples.

7. *To engage students with vivid demonstrations and video clips.* By allowing students to experience principles or findings firsthand, I aim to bring psychology to life. While teaching several introductory psychology sections a year for most of my 29-year career, I have devised or gleaned from others a series of demonstrations that are (a) fairly quick, (b) utterly reliable, (c) dramatic (it doesn't take a statistical caliper to see the effect), (d) pedagogically effective, and (e) just plain fun. Thus, at different times during the semester my students can be found

- squeezing each others' shoulders and ankles (demonstrating psychological measurement principles while measuring the speed of neural transmission),
- befuddled by pseudoparanormal ESP tricks,
- experiencing perceptual adaptation with special glasses that displace the visual field,
- exhibiting common illusory thinking tendencies,
- illustrating group polarization after discussion in small groups.

Nearly every class period also offers one or more brief video clips that enliven lecture and stimulate discussion by bringing the subject matter to life. For example, if we have been considering split-brain research, we watch a split-brain patient being tested. If we have been demonstrating illusory thinking principles, we meet Daniel Kahneman and Amos Tversky on screen.

Finally, I engage my students in active processing of the material through computer simulations created by my colleague, Thomas Ludwig. These are interactive programs that engage the student as experimenter (as when training a rat), as experiment participant (as when being tested on a memory or perceptual illusion task), or as pupil in a dynamic tutorial (that harnesses the computer's graphics potential to teach concepts such as neurotransmission).

Responses to Occasional Comments and Questions

These days all introductory psychology textbooks are alike. Publishers coerce all authors into the same mold. Like writing a sonnet, writing a text allows for freedom within a certain structure. A sonnet has 14 lines in a strict rhythm called *iambic pentameter*. Within this form, poets are free to say what they want. Although text authors are not constrained by so strict a form, tradition and expectation dictate that we organize the discipline into 15 to 20 chapters, beginning with psychology's methods and biological foundations and concluding with social psychology. Within chapters, we must also include certain content, such as Pavlov's and Skinner's work within a chapter on learning. Constrained by this overall organization, each text offers its own voice, level, emphases, examples, and implicit values.

I tell colleagues that if they do not like the overall structure, they should not blame the publishers. As Pogo said, "We have met the enemy and it is us." Publishers assess and produce what the marketplace (i.e., we) wants. When drafting the first edition of my *Social Psychology* I had the idea that American Psychological Association citation style was more appropriate to our professional journals than to textbooks (where parenthetical lists of authors and dates are visual hurdles between sentences). I suggested that we could create a more reader-friendly text that assigned credit using tiny footnotes. My editor was wary, so we agreed to submit the alternative citation styles to a sampling of seven social psychology professors and to live with the survey results. To my disappointment, all but one strongly preferred the traditional professional style, dooming my effort to depart from the conventional structure. Although my editor squelched this little effort to blaze a new trail, she was merely the mouthpiece for my teaching colleagues.

Textbook publishing is a business racket, with publishers piling up huge profits from overpriced books, many of them retreads of old editions with new covers and pictures. Publishers respond that with all the money they invest in producing the text and its free supplements and complimentary copies, their profits are, on average, very thin compared with other businesses. If this is capitalism, it surely is capitalism at its best— with the continuing competition driving us all to higher levels of excellence. The planning for each new edition begins with editors and authors brainstorming on better, more engaging ways to communicate psychology through the text and its teaching package. The authors, meanwhile, continually work at information gathering, before devoting many hundreds of hours to updating their texts, typically with hundreds of new citations—all aiming to give psychology instructors the state-of-the-art presentation that they demand. The ultimate beneficiaries of this competitive process are, of course, our students. Anyone who doubts it should compare current texts and their teaching supports with those published 30 years ago.

Today's dumbed-down texts fail to challenge bright, inquiring students. Today's texts are indeed adapted to today's more inclusive student population. On the 100th anniversary of William James's completion of *Principles of Psychology*, I devoted several weeks of a summer vacation to reading this pioneering text, cover to cover. Time and again I was struck by James's brilliance in anticipating contemporary findings, and I reveled in the elegance of his language. However, this is not a text that my students would relish. Not only was its length massive (1,400 pages), but my computer gave six random passages an average Flesch–Kincaid grade level score of 15.0. By comparison, today's introductory psychology texts average near 11.0, because they have fewer, smaller words per sentence. Readability formulas cannot quantify the substance and depth of ideas, much less the rhythm or vividness of the language. Big ideas can be communicated with clear, crisp prose— indeed, communicated better than with a passive, pedantic voice. "Anything living is easily and naturally expressed in popular language," said Thoreau.

How does one gather all that information and decide what to include? After filing two to three thousand items of information (reprints, manuscripts, abstracts, clippings) culled from journals, convention papers, personal correspondence, and the national press, I pull out the new materials for a given chapter, deal them into topical stacks, then ask of each item: Is this important to the discipline and is it something that an educated person should know about? Within my space limitations, can I effectively communicate this to students? Do I have a place to hang it? If I answer all three questions with yes, I probably will include it. If the answer to any of these questions is no, I probably will not.

Some people, fanning a mammoth book with its two thousand plus citations, are too impressed. I suspect all textbook authors have at times felt like imposters when students or friends have presumed that we knew all that we have written and wrote it the way it now reads. Such reactions by intimidated people—who know that they could never sit down and write a book like that—are mildly embarrassing, because we know that we didn't, either. The book in the lap is actually many mutated drafts removed from what we originally drafted. Thanks to a whole team of reviewers, editors, and production experts (and, in my case, a poet colleague who has been my writing mentor), the finished product is therefore superior to what any author, working alone, is capable of. Although the 1,200-page manuscript that became the book does make an imposing stack, it is less intimidating when viewed as a 3-page-a-day effort (multiplied by 400 days). Although as scholars and writers we often overestimate how much we will accomplish in any given day (and therefore feel frustrated at the day's end), we generally underestimate how much we can accomplish in a year or two, given just a little progress every day.

It must be nice to get all those glowing reviews quoted in marketing brochures. If the truth be known, those aren't all the reviews. Let me divulge some reviews of my texts that you will never see quoted. One reviewer of the first edition manuscript of *Social Psychology* expressed utter contempt for the effort to inject a playful, personal voice, concluding "social psychology is *not* fun and games." A reviewer of my introductory text (who later adopted the book!) offered the following praise in his chapter reviews:

> The use of the English language in this book is atrocious. Faulty grammar and syntax, imprecise meaning and incorrect terminology etc. etc. are abundant. When I'm reading the book I have the feeling that it is written by one of my undergraduate students; when reviewing this edition it is at times like correcting an undergraduate term paper.

In response to another chapter he wrote that "at time this text reads as if it has been a translation from the German language."

Then there was the reviewer who noted that the book "is very biased and opinionated. I don't think the author is very competent. I have thought of writing a text and perhaps now more so," whereupon he proceeded to offer his services.

One of our most difficult professional tasks—whether facing reviews from colleagues or from student evaluations—is being open to the avalanche of criticism without feeling defeated by it. When criticism or rejection gets discouraging, we can take heart from good works that initially went unappreciated. People derided Robert Fulton's steamboat as "Fulton's Folly." As Fulton later said, "Never did a single encouraging remark, a bright hope, a warm wish, cross my path." Much the same reaction greeted the printing press, the telegraph, the incandescent lamp, and the typewriter. John White's (1982) book, *Rejection,* is one story after another of all the scorn and derision that greeted the work of people from Michelangelo and Beethoven to the American poet A. Wilber Stevens, who received back from his hoped-for publisher an envelope of ashes. Dr. Seuss died amidst acclaim recently, long after his work was rejected by some two dozen publishers. "There is no way to sell a book about an unknown Dutch painter," Doubleday explained before Irving Stone's book about Van Gogh survived 15 rejections and sold 25 million copies. In a possibly apocryphal story, one of the seven publishers that rejected *The Tale of Peter Rabbit* said the tale "smelled like rotting carrots."

From my experiences and these cases I derive a lesson: Listen to criticism. Remember that criticism and rejection often serve to dispose of work that deserves to go nowhere. But if, after pondering the criticism, you retain a vision, hold to it. Keep your eye on the goal. As Albert Ellis keeps reminding people, it's okay that not everyone loves what we do. For me, as the years go by and a mountain of praise and criticism has accumulated, compliments have come to provoke less elation and conceit, criticisms less despair and self-disparagement. In retrospect, I am glad I submitted to the process, but I am also glad I did not let it intimidate me into submission.

What is wrong with today's psychology texts? One thing wrong is that their chapters are too long. A modal text has about fifteen 40-page chapters—too long to be read in a single sitting, before the eyes grow weary and the mind wanders. How much better if we were to do as so many economics and biology texts do and parse the material into readable-length chapters—say, forty 15-page chapters.

Alas, like sonnet writers we are constrained by the traditional structure. Even when taking small steps toward shorter chapters (by breaking up childhood and adulthood, sensation and perception, motivation and emotion, and so forth), one hears the frequent complaint: "But my course runs only 15 weeks, and I can't cover more than a chapter per week." This, of course, ignores the length of the chapters. It also ignores the arbitrariness of using the week as a pedagogical unit of time. If a 15-week semester has 45 class sessions, with 40 sessions available for instruction, why not parse the same 600 pages into forty 15-page units (a chapter a day), or twenty 30-page units (a chapter every 2 days)? Again, if the publishers demand a certain structure of authors, it is because we professors demand it of the publishers. The enemy of innovation is us.

What is right with today's psychology texts? Compared with lecture-based teaching (with associated primary source readings), learning from textbooks can offer broader, less idiosyncratic, more representative, and more carefully checked coverage of a discipline. Every introductory text represented by the authors in this volume is vastly superior to their pre-text lectures. Thanks to the magnitude of effort and extensive quality controls, the resulting teaching package is more comprehensive, tightly organized, carefully reviewed, painstakingly edited, efficiently presented, and attractively packaged than any instructor, or even any team of instructors or Web-site managers, could likely home brew. In the spirit of Winston Churchill's remark about democracy, textbooks are the worst way to present information, except for all the others.

By making a discipline's information available to all, textbooks also support a democratic society. Whether one studies at Stanford or Samford, Washtenaw Community College or Washington University, one has access to the same psychology. In their massive review of research, *How College Affects Students*, Ernest Pascarella and Patrick Terenzini (1991, 1994) found that after taking student abilities into account, student learning is little affected by college prestige, library size, and expenditures per student. The similarity of college impacts greatly outweighs their differences. One sure reason is that textbooks—a field's knowledge given away to any and all who will read—serve as the great equalizer.

We take textbooks for granted. But I took them less for granted after receiving a letter that a graduate student put into the hands of an American traveler in Minsk shortly before the breakup of the Soviet Union. Having come into possession of my social psychology text—and it could as well have been any other western text—he wrote with the excitement of a child who just received her first bicycle under the Christmas tree:

> It is the real American book which I come across. That my bad English I difficult to understand everything. I began slowly and with great attention read your book. Even after ferst glance I understood that I discovered the real treasure. Not only I think so. For example, my scientific superviser Professor Colominsky, vise-president Soviety Psychology Society, when I shower it to him enthusiastically shook it over his head and exclaimed, "Look everybody what a beautiful book. Look everybody!!!" Ind one of my colleague told me: I have a black envy, I shall try to steal this book from you. She joked, but to be on the safe side I hid my treasure. . . . I spend a lot of time everyday reading "Social Psychology" like a little child with its favourite toy. But such as I am not child (I am 24 years old) I do hope that with the help of your wonderful book I shall get deeper understanding of psychology and that it will contribute immensely to my scientific background. . . . I thank God for so lucky present. . . .

A couple of years later, as I devoted 4 days to hosting his mentor, Yakov Kolominsky, then vice president of the Soviet Psychological Society, I was struck not only by the curtain of ignorance that has separated our two worlds of psychology, not only by their hunger for professional contacts and exchange with those of us in the West, but also by our enormous good fortune in having been blessed here in North America with everything from free and easy access to information to not having to spend hours each week accumulating life's necessities.

Professing psychology surely is a high calling. What more fascinating subject could we study and teach than our own human workings? What topics are more in need of critical analysis than those on which psychological science shines its light? What academic subject is more influential in shaping values and lifestyles than the young science of psychology? What vocation is more mind expanding, full of fresh surprises, and focused on humanly significant questions? When tempted to grumble about our workloads, our reward systems, or our students, let us pause to remember: To be teaching psychology in our time, in our places, is a privilege we ought not take for granted.

References

Marty, M. (1988, December 1). Graceful prose: Your good deed for the day. *Context*, p. 2.

Miller, G. A. (1969). Psychology as a means of promoting human welfare. *American Psychologist, 24,* 1063–1075.

Pascarella, E. T., & Terenzini, P. T. (1991). *How college affects students: Findings and insights from twenty years of research.* San Francisco: Jossey-Bass.

Pascarella, E. T., & Terenzini, P. T. (1994, January/February). Living with myths: Undergraduate education in America. *Change,* pp. 28–32.

Peterson, E. (1992). *Under the unpredictable plant.* Grand Rapids, MI: Eerdmans.

White, J. (1982). *Rejection.* Boston: Addison-Wesley.

Rod Plotnik

Model for Being an Effective Instructor

8

For many of us, our first semester of teaching was like walking through fire, and our main goal became surviving and not getting burned too badly by our mistakes. When that first semester or quarter ended, we licked our wounds, learned from our mistakes, changed our policies, and hoped we would do better the next time. This process of learning how to be an effective instructor often takes years of personal trial and error, because graduate programs offer little training or supervision in effective teaching and rarely provide a practicum in teaching.

The issues involving how to be an effective instructor became very real to me when, about 15 years ago, I was appointed supervisor of the department's 10–12 teaching assistants, who were either first- or second-year master's students. Although teaching assistants at many other universities usually grade papers or conduct discussion groups, our teaching assistants are assigned two introductory psychology classes and are actually responsible for giving lectures, writing exams, and dealing with students' problems. Just as parents try to save their children from making the mistakes they made, I wanted to save these new teaching assistants from making the same mistakes that I had suffered through. But what exactly would I tell new instructors, and equally important, how could I be sure that they would follow my advice? To answer these questions, I took the only sure step that I knew. I turned our introductory psychology classrooms into teaching laboratories.

Turning the Classroom Into a Teaching Laboratory

I began with three basic questions: How does one select teaching assistants who are most likely to develop into good instructors? Can one give new instructors proven class materials instead of asking them to develop their own? How does one determine whether new instructors are actually following the good advice and avoiding the mistakes generally made by inexperienced instructors?

Because my previous research had involved observing and coding the social and emotional behaviors of primates, I was very familiar with doing observational research. Furthermore, because I had learned the importance of evaluating behaviors by using videotaped recordings, I made videotaping a high priority. However, the first time I asked the new instructors to be videotaped I was given a surprise. The second-year teaching assistants, whom I had inherited and who had not been videotaped their previous year, all found reasons or made excuses to avoid being videotaped in their classrooms. The first-year teaching assistants agreed because they assumed it was part of the training program. These first-year teaching assistants were nervous about being videotaped, but interestingly enough, they were also curious to see themselves and wanted to get ideas from watching their peers.

In addition to using videotapes to evaluate new instructors' in-class teaching, I also used student numerical evaluations and written comments (Marsh, 1984). Finally, I was able to compare my ratings of the teaching assistants' videotapes with their student evaluations. From this kind of observational research I identified many of the practical skills, personality traits, and classroom environments that resulted in effective instruction. I organized these observations into a three-component model for effective teaching, which I use in my two-semester course Practicum in Teaching.

Model for Effective Teaching

The model (see Figure 1) is essentially a checklist of behaviors in three different but interrelated areas that are important for being an effective instructor. The advantage of this model is that it identifies three areas in which new instructors need training and specifies which practical skills need to be developed. Thinking through this three-component model also helped me identify behaviors that needed improve-

FIGURE 1

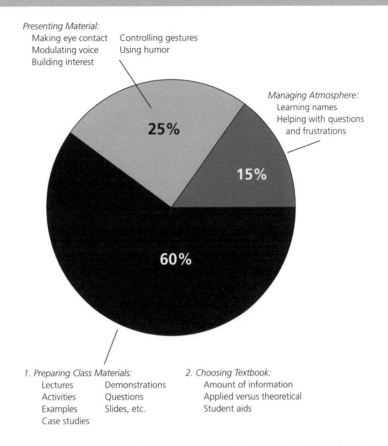

Presenting Material:
Making eye contact   Controlling gestures
Modulating voice   Using humor
Building interest

Managing Atmosphere:
Learning names
Helping with questions
and frustrations

1. *Preparing Class Materials:*
    Lectures   Demonstrations
    Activities   Questions
    Examples   Slides, etc.
    Case studies

2. *Choosing Textbook:*
    Amount of information
    Applied versus theoretical
    Student aids

The three-component model (60% preparing class materials and choosing textbook, 15% managing classroom atmosphere, and 25% presenting material) identifies three interrelated areas important for successful teaching and specifies the practical behaviors beginning teachers need to master to become effective instructors. The model was developed from observation research on new instructors.

ment, even though I had believed that with my years of experience, I knew all there was to know about teaching.

COMPONENT 1: PREPARING CLASS MATERIALS AND CHOOSING A TEXTBOOK

I estimated that preparing class materials made up about 60% of what an instructor must do to be effective (as shown in Figure 1). Preparing well-organized and interesting class materials is a real problem for most new instructors, who lack the time, knowledge, and experience. I found that even when new instructors were given detailed instructions on how to prepare interesting class materials, most of them essentially repeated the material in the textbook, perhaps adding an example or two.

Much of my time as supervisor has been devoted to developing, writing, and organizing class materials; testing them in the classroom; and then revising them until they are proven effective. Such development and testing of class materials, which involves interweaving information with examples, case studies, questions, activities, or a video, slide, or transparency is extremely time-consuming. I found that creating and integrating materials for a 50-minute class usually required from 10–20 hours. I am sure that the preparation of class materials would be even more time-consuming if I were not already familiar with new research findings, examples, case studies, videos, movies, and activities that I discover during regular revisions of my textbook (Plotnik, 1996a). I seriously doubt that new instructors, who are simultaneously trying to establish a research program, could devote 10–20 hours to develop excellent materials for each class.

One solution to this problem is for experienced instructors to give new instructors proven class materials so that we stop inventing this particular wheel. I have found that nothing boosts the confidence and self-esteem of new instructors like using proven materials. How much more confident teaching assistants feel when they walk into class with proven materials than when using material they tried to prepare the previous evening.

Choosing a Textbook

The textbook sets the tone and atmosphere for the entire class and determines the amount of knowledge students will take from the class. In choosing a text, there are two primary considerations: (a) the amount of content covered and (b) the amount of time time needed to make the content interesting.

What role should the text play? Perhaps most of us who teach introductory psychology would agree that a text should cover the classic experiments but also discuss new and exciting developments in the field. Texts can be grouped into two general classes: those of about 650–750 pages of information (excluding prefaces, table of contents, glossaries, appendices, permissions, and references) and those that have about 500–650 pages. There are advantages and disadvantages to choosing a text from these two general classes.

650- to 750-Page Texts

The principal advantage of these texts is that they cover an incredible amount of information, and the instructor can be assured that material that hasn't been discussed in class is covered in the text. Another advantage is that these texts provide a good resource or encyclopedia of the entire field of psychology. The principal disadvantage of these texts is that students are exposed to so much information that they often feel overwhelmed and incapable of deciding which information is most important. (For example, is a classic but discarded theory—Sheldon's body types—important to learn?) In addition, attempting to cover 650–750 pages of information in one semester leaves little time for integrating examples, videos, case studies, and other activities that make the material and the class more interesting. These longer texts are more appropriate for a yearlong course, and some of them remedy this by providing brief editions that are more appropriate for a one-semester or one-quarter course. Many new instructors may not realize, however, that the quickest way to take the interest and excitement out of an introductory psychology class is to overwhelm students with too much material.

500- to 650-Page Texts

These texts are by design more selective in what they cover and more manageable for a one-semester or quarter-semester course. The principal advantage of these shorter texts is that their amount of information does not overwhelm the students or make them unclear about what is important. In addition, these shorter texts leave the instructor more time for integrating examples, videos, and activities to make the material more interesting. The principal disadvantage of these texts is that they are more selective and may, therefore, fail to cover some of the instructor's favorite studies.

Coverage or Interest?

One of the major problems in teaching introductory psychology is deciding between how much to cover and how much time to devote to making information interesting. As instructors we often assume that students will be or should be intellectually excited by a concept, theory, or experiment. However, we discover that many students are not excited by concepts but rather need engaging examples to make the concepts come alive. For example, it is not uncommon to meet former students who still remember an interesting story or example that was used to illustrate some concept or idea (Bernstein, 1994). One of the greatest challenges for a textbook author is to be able to link examples and material in such a way that students will remember the material. Whatever your philosophy on the role of a textbook, the current market offers a number of very good texts.

COMPONENT 2: PRESENTING MATERIALS

I estimated that presenting class material makes up about 25% of the tasks an instructor must perform to be effective. Presenting skills include being enthusiastic; modulating one's voice; speaking slowly; making eye contact; controlling extraneous or distracting gestures; being able to make examples, cases, or stories come to life; and having (developing) a sense of humor. Although some instructors consider presentation skills to be pedagogical tools that have little place in the college classroom, videotapes and student evaluations indicate otherwise. Some of the best class materials quickly lose their interest and effectiveness when presented poorly. Neglecting the impact of presentation skills is the primary mistake made by new teaching assistants. Their confidence and self-esteem plummet when students respond to their presentations with lack of interest. Presentation skills can be enhanced by certain dispositional personality traits, which brings us to the issue of selecting instructors.

It should be no surprise to learn that new teaching assistants who are energetic, outgoing, and friendly very quickly develop into effective instructors, as reflected both by student evaluations and from their videotapes. New teaching assistants who are shy, reticent, and socially reserved rarely achieve equivalent success in the same time period. If one can select from a pool of potential instructors, those who are highly motivated and full of energy and enthusiasm will be best suited to make the class material come alive and interest the wide range of students who enroll in these courses.

IMPORTANCE OF VIDEOTAPED PRACTICE AND FEEDBACK

Even if it has been possible to select new instructors who are energetic, outgoing, and friendly, most of them still need at least two semesters of videotaped practice and feedback to develop good presentation skills.

As I noted earlier, I have found it critical to provide new instructors with proven materials for the first five or six class periods. Even so, I discovered that these proven materials were not being presented in an effective way. For example, for their very first class, I provide teaching assistants with interesting vignettes that introduce the major areas of psychology and require from 15 to 20 minutes to present. I require the teaching assistants to memorize these vignettes and be prepared to deliver them with interest and enthusiasm. I also tell them to speak slowly, emphasize certain phrases, build excitement, make eye contact, and refrain from pacing back and forth. Still, they all make these mistakes the first time they role-play in front of their peers.

I tell them in a friendly and supportive way to try again, and this time try even harder to speak slowly, be more enthusiastic, make eye contact, and not pace. Almost invariably, their second performance is an exact repeat of all of their first mistakes! And they usually protest, "But I was doing what you suggested." It is only when I play back their videotapes and they see their performances do they realize what they were doing. At last they see and often explain, "Yes, I was speaking too fast and not making eye contact and sounded sort of boring."

It usually requires four to six videotaped practice sessions with feedback before new teaching assistants noticeably improve their presentation skills. However, their improvement is often so dramatic that their peers break into spontaneous applause. I think it would be helpful if all instructors, both new and experienced, realized the impact that presentation skills have on making class materials more or less interesting. Needless to say, good presentation skills are almost impossible to develop without videotaped practice and feedback.

COMPONENT 3: MANAGING CLASSROOM ATMOSPHERE

I estimated that managing classroom atmosphere made up about 15% of what an instructor must do to be effective. Initially I had not consciously thought about my classroom atmosphere or what I might do to improve it. However, after monitoring my own behavior and watching videotapes of the teaching assistants, I found that there were three specific areas that could create an atmosphere more conducive to learning: helping students answer questions, helping students deal with frustration and failure of exams, and taking an interest in students by learning their names.

Helping Students Answer Questions

One way to determine whether students understand the concepts or terms that have been explained is to ask questions. However, many students feel uncomfortable when asked questions, because some may be shy, some do not know the answer, or some may even remember being embarrassed in the past when failing to answer a question correctly.

Many of us can remember our own experiences of being embarrassed and feeling humiliated when failing to answer a question correctly and being passed over with the words, "No, that's not correct." Consequently, many of us soon learned ways to avoid being asked questions, such as staring at the floor or putting our heads down and pretending to be taking notes. After much trial and error, I discovered three easy but effective techniques that help students answer questions correctly and avoid feeling embarrassed or humiliated.

- Spell out the answer. Suppose I asked this question: "If you were going to remove a single area of brain that would make a person lose all senses except smell, which area would you remove?" Because I have already discussed this brain area, my question serves as a check and review. However, because this question asks the students to apply the information they learned, many have difficulty answering it. If the student has difficulty answering, I begin to write out the answer on the blackboard and ask him or her to shout out the answer as soon as they know it. I begin to write, T H A L , and right about here the student shouts out, "thalamus," because he or she *did* know the answer. Students like this technique because it not only helps them answer the question but also demonstrates that they really did know the answer (with a little help). If this technique is used regularly, students who have difficulty answering will often say, "Start writing it on the board."
- Give multiple choices. A second technique that is equally effective is to ask a question and as soon as you see the student having trouble, explain that you will give them three choices. I always make two of the three choices so absurd (stomach, thalamus, gall bladder) that the student cannot help but select the correct answer. Students usually laugh at the absurd and incorrect alternatives and happily select the correct answer.
- Have only two alternatives. A third technique to help students answer questions is to phrase them so that the students are given two alternatives and have a 50% chance of answering correctly. If students choose the wrong alternative, I ask them to try again. They usually laugh and then give the correct answer.

More experienced faculty are often reluctant to try these techniques. They sometimes feel that these techniques are too simplistic to be effective, are more appropriate for high school than college students, and that college students need to learn to deal with public embarrassment and frustration. However, new teaching assistants who start off using these techniques the first day of class find them very effective in engaging student interest, decreasing student embarrassment, and improving the classroom atmosphere. After these techniques have been used for 2 to 4 weeks, the classroom environment visibly changes into a friendly atmosphere in which students are eager to participate in activities, ask questions, and try to answer questions without fear of being embarrassed or humiliated.

Helping Students Deal With Frustration and Failure of Exams

Students who do less well on exams than expected often become frustrated and angry, and their first reaction is often to blame the instructor for writing a tricky, unfair, or too difficult exam. The more challenging and thought provoking the questions, the more likely they will be to generate frustration and anger. One obvious but not very educationally appealing solution is to give relatively easy exams, which result in good grades and general grade inflation for many students.

Another solution is to continue to give fair but challenging questions but work on changing the students' attribution regarding blame and responsibility. For example, instead of blaming teachers for their poorer than expected performance or getting angry at test questions, we help students see that our questions are generally fair and that getting angry at us or our exams will not improve their future performance. We use an attribution procedure that I originally developed for my own classes. I found it so effective that I passed it on to my teaching assistants, who have had equal success.

Immediately before giving back each exam, we spend about 10–15 minutes discussing three points:

- Blame:

    It is easy to look around the classroom and find the one person whom you think is chiefly responsible for your doing less well than you hoped. Of course, that one person is me. But before you blame me, there are a couple of things to consider. Many of the very questions that you missed, other students got right. Many students got As and Bs. A number of students even scored above 95%. Because many students did well on this exam and answered some of the very questions that you missed, it doesn't make a lot of sense to blame me or my questions for your performance. Instead, try to figure out how you might improve your study skills, or come and talk to me about what you might do.

• Anger and frustration:

If you didn't get the grade you wanted or think you deserved, there is a natural tendency to feel frustrated and perhaps get angry at me and my questions. Perhaps you believe that because you read the material two or three times and took good notes and studied hard, you deserve a better grade than you received. But you may be forgetting that some students may have had more time to study than you, or have developed better memories, or retain more information, or aren't bothered as much by test anxiety. You can see that there are many reasons why other students may have scored higher than you. Instead of getting angry at me or my questions, you may want to think about why other students scored higher. Perhaps you need to begin studying earlier, get help taking notes, or form a study group. Think about channeling your anger and frustration into developing new study plans that will help you improve on your performance on the next exam.

• No arguments:

I'm going to pass your exams back and let you look over the questions that you have missed. I don't want to argue about questions, but if you raise your hand, I'll come by and explain why a question is right or wrong. Now, if you think your answer is correct, even though it is marked wrong, write out a case for your answer and hand it in with the exam. If your thinking is good, I'll give you an additional point.

Most instructors discover that allowing students to argue over questions in class turns very mean very quickly. The result is that students become very angry and instructors become very defensive, which makes students even angrier. Our solution to prevent arguments is to allow students to write out cases that show their thinking. In a class of 50 students, we typically receive from three to six cases, and about half of them demonstrate good thinking and deserve additional points. New teaching assistants have an especially difficult time dealing with in-class arguments. This procedure eliminates that problem, but allows students a means to make their cases in a much calmer fashion.

• Bad mood:

After getting a bad exam back in college, I would find someone else who also got a poor grade and we would complain together and remain in bad moods. Even worse, when I got to my apartment, I would tell my roommate about my bad exam and this would put me back into a bad mood. So, if your grade puts you into a bad mood, give yourself 20 minutes to feel bad and do your complaining. Then, pick yourself up and do something or think something pleasant and enjoyable to get out of this bad mood. Remember that even your best friends will soon tire of your bad mood. Staying in a bad mood is very hard on your mental and physical health, so try to get into a good mood as quickly as you can.

New teaching assistants role-play giving this attribution speech, so that they give it in a way that is friendly and supportive but not condescending. Our procedure is to repeat this speech (in slightly different ways) before giving back each exam (total of four exams).

Our success in changing students' attribution toward our questions and exams can be easily measured by students' responses to Question 5 on teacher evaluation forms. Student were asked to rate the "extent to which the testing process (examinations, problem assignments, papers, etc.) contributed to your learning the subject matter," on a 5-point scale where 5 represented the highest possible score. When we did not use the attribution speech, students generally gave Question 5 a rating of 3; when we used the attribution speech, student ratings on this question were raised to 4.

As one faculty member remarked, "The harder you and your teaching assistants grade, the more your students like you." Again, whether instructors use this or other attribution procedures will depend on how active a role they wish to take in managing the emotional interactions in their classrooms.

Learning Students' Names

When students are asked what they like about their instructors, they will often mention that the instructor took the time to learn their names. Learning the names of 45–50 students usually takes teaching assistants about 3–6 weeks and results in a very friendly atmosphere. Knowing students' names allows new instructors to more easily ask questions and encourage participation in class discussions and class activities. Learning students' names also allows instructors to identify shy students who need extra support to answer questions. Students really appreciate teaching assistants for making the effort to learn their names. This relatively easy technique is one of the quickest and most effective ways to create a friendly classroom environment.

From observing videotapes of my own classes as well as those of my teaching assistants, I have found that there is a clear difference between the energy level and interactions that take place in a friendly class environment versus one that is more formal. In a friendly atmosphere students are much more relaxed, eager to participate and answer questions, and engage in class activities with very little fear of being embarrassed or humiliated. In a very real sense, it is much easier to teach in a friendly class environment.

PREDICTIONS FROM THE THREE-COMPONENT MODEL

We can use the three-component model to identify and predict how different components will affect performance in the classroom as well as student and instructor attitudes.

- Instructors who are very good at preparing class materials but less capable at presenting materials or managing their classrooms will never be fully appreciated for their efforts and never receive the student evaluations they think they deserve. These experienced instructors are likely to doubt the validity of student evaluations because they are obviously preparing good materials but receiving lower than expected evaluations. One solution to this problem is to recognize the importance of the other two components (presenting and managing) and perhaps use videotape feedback and support from master instructors or faculty mentors to improve these other components (Murray, 1995b).

- New instructors who are dispositionally shy, soft-spoken, and reticent will face a greater challenge in developing effective classroom instruction. Without help from master instructors or faculty mentors, dispositionally shy instructors may find teaching a very frustrating experience. I have found that teaching assistants who are slow to develop good presentation and management skills are continually frustrated by the lack of student interest in lectures.

- Good presentation and management skills will not compensate for poorly prepared class materials. For example, one teaching assistant who was exceptionally good at presentation of materials and management of the classroom asked if he could have a very informal class in which students asked or discussed anything related to psychology. In his evaluations, students commented that he was an interesting and friendly person but much too disorganized and unprepared in his lectures. They found his class enjoyable but not instructive. Thus, presentation and management skills alone will not result in having great classes unless these skills are used to present well-prepared class materials.

- Instructors who have dispositional traits (energetic, outgoing, friendly, enthusiastic) that lend themselves to presenting materials and managing class atmosphere well quickly develop into very good instructors, provided they are given proven and interesting class materials and receive videotaped practice and feedback. This group of new instructors usually receives higher scores on student evaluations than more experienced faculty, despite the use of rigorous grading standards.

For example, the mean student evaluations of 14 teaching assistants in spring 1995 at San Diego State University was 4.4 (5.0 being best), compared with 4.3 for regular faculty teaching lower division courses, 4.1 for regular faculty teaching upper division courses, and 4.1 for regular faculty teaching graduate courses. Similar results were reported at the University of New Hampshire, where graduate teaching assistants who took a practicum in teaching received higher scores on student evaluations than did the regular faculty (Fernald, 1995).

Finally, note the skills that award-winning instructors possess. For example, the 1995 American Psychological Association Division 2 annual teaching award for 4-year college and university professor was awarded to Mitchell Handelsman of the University of Colorado, Denver. Professor Handelsman was acknowledged for his use of case studies, debates, class presentations, role-playing, demonstrations, questionnaires, and other methods to help students study psychology by *doing* psychology; his sense of humor and accessibility; and his concern and respect for students (*Teaching of Psychology*, 1995). There is no question that Professor Handelsman excels in the three components of teaching: preparing materials, presenting materials, and managing his class environment.

Class Activities Versus Lectures

National surveys of U.S. college and university faculty indicate that the lecture format is still the most often used teaching method (Finkelstein, 1995). About 80% of college instructors reported that they preferred the lecture format because of its usefulness in simplifying and focusing on what is important in the ever-increasing amount of information provided in psychology texts (Finkelstein, 1995). Although the lecture format is very popular, there are a number of equally good and perhaps better ways of providing information, specifically class activities that require more student participation (Bernstein, 1994). When we think of class activities, a major concern is that they may be fun for the students but fail to cover important concepts, terms, or theories. To avoid this problem, I set two general criteria for developing a class activity: The activity must require full student participation, and the goal of the activity must be to teach students to learn and understand the important concepts and terms.

Procedure for Class Activities

1. Before the class activity, students are instructed to read the assigned material, take 2–3 pages of notes, and bring their notes to the next class. Students who bring notes to class receive points for doing so and can take part in the activity. Students without notes become spectators.

2. On the day of the activity, students are divided into groups of 4–7 students. Although they work together in groups, each group chooses one spokesperson who answers for the group.

3. Each activity includes a number of rounds in which each group has a chance to answer questions and earn points. At the end of the activity, points are totaled. Each member of the first-, second-, third-, and fourth-place groups receives points that count toward final grades.

Kinds of Class Activities

So far I have developed five different class activities that meet the two criteria: They have proven effective in involving the students and cover the assigned material (Plotnik, 1993, 1994, 1996b). In other words, these activities are not extra fun-and-games but an integral part of the material. What follows is a short description of each activity.

1. Brain game: Basic anatomy and function. This activity turns students into brain scientists who must identify a specific area of the brain based on a set of physical symptoms. This activity has undergone a number of revisions and is now our most popular activity. By the end of the class, students have identified the major areas of the brain. Students much prefer being involved in identifying brain areas rather than just hearing about them in the more traditional lecture format.

2. Jeopardy: Major terms in motivation and emotion. This activity is modeled after the well-known television show and is our second most popular activity. We use Jeopardy for motivation and emotion because this material tends to be more theoretical and less interesting to the students. However, the Jeopardy format can be used for any material and serves as a good way to review material. However, be advised that students take this game very seriously, so the rules must be clearly specified and followed.

3. Stormy childhood: Infancy and childhood development. Students are given a short story that details the problems a single mother encounters in raising her daughter. The story is written to describe and include developmental terms, concepts, and theories (Freud's, Piaget's, and Erikson's stages; newborn senses, motor development, emotional development, etc.). Students must link the description or explanation in the story with the correct developmental terms.

4. Social game: Newspaper stories illustrating social concepts. Headlines and their accompanying stories are taken from

recent newspaper articles. Students must identify which terms or concepts (prejudice, discrimination, stereotype, attribution) are described in the newspaper stories. This is also a very popular activity because it shows that social psychology is something we encounter daily.

5. Movies: Identifying abnormal behaviors. We show brief segments from movies that illustrate some unusual or abnormal behaviors, such as the scene of Robin Williams's character hallucinating in the movie *The Fisher King*. Students are first asked to identify the symptoms and the disorder. They are then asked to discuss the psychological or pharmacological treatment for the disorder. This is also a very popular activity because the movie scenes are often dramatic and intrinsically interesting.

Over 90% of our students (about 1,000 per semester) read the assigned material, take notes, and bring the notes to class so they can participate in these activities and earn points that count toward their final grades.

We have asked students to rate the usefulness of these activities on their final class evaluations. The vast majority of students give high marks to these activities. Representative comments include, "The games helped me greatly in learning the material." "The games helped me get to know the people in class and the material we needed to learn!" "The games helped me prepare for tests and understand the material better." "The games were great for making the information concrete." "The games were a good learning technique."

Although each of these five class activities required about 15–20 hours to develop, I am working with colleagues to develop more because they have proven so effective in involving students in the material. Students prefer these class activities to their more passive role in traditional lectures, which primarily entails listening and taking notes. Students' performance on exams indicates that these class activities are just as effective as lectures in helping students learn the assigned material.

How Well Does Graduate School Prepare New Instructors?

Although there are some graduate schools around the country that have practicums in teaching, many have only started to offer this course within the past 5 years (Fernald, 1995; Perlman, 1994).

However, graduate practicums in teaching seem to be more the exception than the rule. I discovered the absence of practicums in teaching while interviewing finalists for a position at San Diego State University in the winter of 1994. I gave 30–60 minute telephone interviews to 11 new PhDs, all from well-known universities. The majority of my questions focused on teaching, including kind of preparation, first experiences in the classroom, and amount of mentoring. Typically, these applicants had begun by assisting a professor in running a laboratory, grading papers, or leading discussion groups. Then, in their third or fourth years, they were assigned to teach one or more courses in their particular areas. Here's what most of the PhD candidates said about their training in teaching and their first experiences in the classroom:

- They were given little or no training in how to prepare class material, present information, or manage the classroom environment. Whatever pedagogical techniques they learned, they did so through their own trial and error.
- Most believed it was important to cover as much material as possible, even if they had to rush through the material at the end of a lecture or at the end of the course. Many said they had to omit material the second time around.
- Most initially chose textbooks that were too difficult for their students and changed textbooks the next time.
- Most remarked that their first semester was pretty awful (trial by fire, walking through land mines, barely staying afloat) for which they were ill prepared.
- Almost all enjoyed teaching and wanted to be good instructors but wished that they had been better prepared for teaching while in graduate school.

Perhaps one reason that most universities do not have a practicum in teaching is the well-known double standard concerning research and teaching.

Psychology's Double Standard

The double standard for research and teaching is subtly indoctrinated during graduate school and is reinforced and perpetuated with some of the following well-known and often repeated phrases:

"Research gets you promoted, teaching doesn't."

"Research will make your reputation, teaching won't."

"You only have so much time and energy, so be smart and put it into research."

"Steal time from teaching and put it into research."

"Get a grant so you can teach less."

"Only those who can't do research end up teaching."

That the double standard is alive and well comes from a recent survey in which 78% of 103 faculty respondents said that evidence of research skill is more important in making decisions about hiring than evidence of teaching skills. Twenty-five years ago, teaching skills were rated as more important. In addition, 65% agreed that new college professors often experienced adjustment problems because their graduate training had not prepared them for teaching (Perlman, 1994). A related national survey of faculty at 4-year colleges and universities reported that virtually all had received advanced training in an academic field but virtually none received any pedagogical training (Finkelstein, 1995).

In an attempt to change psychology's double standard concerning teaching and research, both the American Psychological Society and the American Psychological Association have begun to schedule conferences on teaching at their national conventions. Perhaps these organizations will use their influence to persuade graduate programs to establish practicums in teaching so that their new PhDs will be as competently trained in teaching as they now are in research. Of course, the ultimate solution is a doctoral degree in teaching psychology (similar to the PsyD) that would formally recognize the importance of training effective instructors.

Finally, there has been renewed discussion of the need to recognize and reward good teaching at both the departmental and national levels. We can only hope that college and university administrations will take appropriate actions to reward good instructors in the same way they reward good researchers (Mac Iver, Reuman, & Main, 1995; Murray, 1995a).

References

Bernstein, D. A. (1994, July–August). The merits of classroom demonstrations. *APS Observer*.

Fernald, P. S. (1995). Preparing psychology graduate students for the professoriate. *American Psychologist, 50*, 421–427.

Finkelstein, M. J. (1995). College faculty as teachers. *The NEA Almanac of higher education* (pp. 33–47). Washington, DC: National Education Association.

Mac Iver, D. A., Reuman, D. A., & Main, S. R. (1995). Social structuring of the school: Studying what is, illuminating what could be. *Annual Review of Psychology, 46,* 375–400.

Marsh, H. W. (1984). Students' evaluations of university teaching: Dimensionality, reliability, validity, potential biases, and utility. *Journal of Educational Psychology, 76,* 707–754.

Murray, B. (1995a, December). Good teaching often goes unrewarded. *APA Monitor,* p. 40.

Murray, B. (1995b, September). New faculty get boost partnering with senior staff. *APA Monitor,* p. 50

Perlman, B. (1994). *TA training in psychology—1994 survey* (Survey feedback). Oshkosh: University of Wisconsin.

Plotnik, R. (1993, January). *Introducing students to psychology: Activities, demonstrations, and examples.* Paper presented at the 15th Annual National Institute on the Teaching of Psychology, St. Petersburg Beach, FL.

Plotnik, R. (1994, April). *Making your classroom interactive.* Paper presented at the 74th Annual Convention of the Western Psychological Association, Hilo, Hawaii.

Plotnik, R. (1996a). *Introduction to psychology* (4th ed.). Pacific Grove, NJ: Brooks/Cole.

Plotnik, R. (1996b, January). *Turning lectures into activities in introductory psychology.* Paper presented at the 18th Annual National Institute on the Teaching of Psychology, St. Petersburg Beach, FL.

Teaching of Psychology. (1995). 1995 Teaching Award winners. *Teaching of Psychology, 22,* 164–168.

Robert J. Sternberg

Teaching Students to Think as Psychologists

9

t started with a *C* in introductory psychology. It might have ended there. I went to college eager to major in psychology. I was excited at last to be able to fulfill my dream and start the study of psychology my freshman year. The dream quickly became a nightmare. I didn't like the course; it apparently didn't like me either. Nor did the professor: In handing back one of my papers, he commented that there was a famous Sternberg in psychology, and apparently there wasn't about to be another. Point made. I switched intended majors.

Fortunately, I switched to mathematics. I took the introduction to real analysis course for future math majors and discovered that I was actually worse in pure math than I was in psychology. Back to psychology, where I ended up getting better grades in upper level courses and graduating with highest honors in psychology.

I was lucky I tried math, because this utter fiasco encouraged me to switch back to what I really enjoyed— psychology. But how many students bomb the introductory course; conclude, as I did, that they don't have the interest in or the ability to pursue psychology; and then switch to

The work reported herein was supported under the Javits Act program (Grant #R206R50001) as administered by the Office of Educational Research and Improvement, U.S. Department of Education. The findings and opinions expressed in this report do not reflect the positions or policies of the Office of Educational Research and Improvement or the U.S. Department of Education.

137

another major? Quite a few, I suspect. These students end up study-ing something else that may interest them, more or less, but perhaps quite a bit less than psychology would have. So they lose. And the field loses too: People who might have become good or even excellent psy-chologists are lost to another field. In my own case, had I switched to almost anything but math, I would probably still be working in that area today, perhaps only mildly interested in what I was doing rather than wildly enthusiastic, as indeed I am.

There is a flip side to this phenomenon—the students who are excel-lent memory learners but who don't have some of the other skills that are necessary for being a good psychologist. They go on to graduate school, get As in their course work, but show little imagination in for-mulating theories or designing experiments or perhaps few interpersonal skills in patient care. If all of psychology were like the introductory course, these students would be fine, but that's not the way the field is.

Ask yourself, as I have asked myself many times, how often, as a professional psychologist, you have needed to do what led to success in your introductory course? The answer is likely to be "rarely" or "never." In 21 years of teaching and research, I've never once had to memorize a book or a lecture, or take a multiple-choice test, for that matter. Too often, what is required for success in the introductory (and low-level) courses bears no resemblance to what is required for suc-cess in the field. The result is, perhaps, that some of the "wrong" peo-ple go into the field, and some of the "right" ones leave it.

Why might such a phenomenon be a common one? Because most introductory psychology courses emphasize memory learning. Stu-dents learn the major facts and concepts and then receive multiple-choice and short-answer tests assessing their recall and recognition of these facts and concepts. Of course, there is nothing wrong with learn-ing the fundamentals of the field. Every psychologist has to know them. But how many of the facts and concepts that you learned in introductory psychology are still at the center, or even the periphery, of the field? The field moves so fast that the factual material in the textbooks of today bears almost no resemblance to the factual mater-ial in the book, say, from which I studied (in 1968). Whatever it is that we want students to learn, almost certainly it is not material that will quickly go out of date. What, then, do we want students to learn?

I would argue that the main goal of the introductory psychology course should be to teach students to think as psychologists. Why? Those who become psychologists will have a start toward understand-ing the kinds of thinking they will need in order to proceed and suc-ceed in their chosen fields. And the much larger number who do not become psychologists will carry something away from the course that will be valuable to them for the rest of their lives: the metacognitive knowledge of how to take a psychological perspective on problems. When they confront problems, whether in their work or in their personal lives, they will be able, at least to some extent, to think about these problems the way a psychologist would. What else is a liberal education about? Really, it's about learning to think from a great variety of perspectives, including our own as psychologists. So what do students need to be able to do in order to think as psychologists?

Acquisition of a Knowledge Base

To become good psychological thinkers, students need to master some of the basic facts and concepts of the discipline. We have passed through the 1960s—with the "new" math, the "new" physics, and the "new" chemistry—in which we mistakenly believed that students could become good thinkers with a minimal knowledge base. Now we know better (Chi, Glaser, & Farr, 1988). To think as psychologists, students need to master the fundamentals of the discipline.

Having stated the importance of knowledge base, I need further to emphasize that what distinguishes expert from novice thinkers in a given field is not so much the extent of the knowledge base but, rather, its organization (Chi, Glaser, & Rees, 1982; Chi & Koeske, 1983; Larkin, McDermott, Simon, & Simon, 1980). Thus, emphasizing disconnected memory learning, as some courses still do, probably won't fill the bill. Students need to learn to see the interconnections of what they are learning and then fit this new information into their already existing knowledge base (Mayer & Greeno, 1972).

Students taking introductory courses and studying for final examinations often end up mindlessly rehearsing material, without encoding the material in any depth; as a result, they spend the time to learn it but do not learn it well (Baddeley, 1986; Craik & Tulving, 1975; Tulving, 1983). It is important, therefore, that students *learn how to learn* the material, so that they will not, rather quickly, forget it, if they ever indeed do learn it.

Triarchic Learning and Thinking

Students need to be taught to think in at least three different ways with the fundamentals of psychology—analytically, creatively, and practically (Sternberg, 1985, 1994b, 1995, 1997). Analytical thinking involves comparing and contrasting, judging, evaluating, and critiquing. Psychologists think analytically when they review articles (including their own), critique experiments, evaluate theories, or assess the nature of a client's problems. Creative thinking involves creating, inventing, discovering, imagining, and supposing. Psychologists think creatively when they formulate theories, design experiments or creative lesson plans, see connections between disparate kinds of research, and propose treatment plans. Practical thinking involves applying, using, and utilizing. Psychologists think practically when they try to plan a lecture so that it will be understandable by their students, write grant proposals in ways to maximize the probability of obtaining funding, interact with clients in ways to elicit the nature of the clients' problems, and design experiments so that the experiments are more likely to work out.

Good teaching in psychology—or in any other field (Sternberg, 1994a)—involves (a) giving students opportunities to think in these three ways and (b) modeling these kinds of thinking for the students. Both of these techniques of instruction are important.

Students need opportunities to think triarchically. They will not truly learn to think analytically, creatively, and practically unless they do so actively. It is not enough for them to read examples in their texts or to hear examples in lectures. As we all know, it is one thing to be able passively to understand how someone else thinks about a problem and another to be able actively to think this way oneself (see essays by Baron & Sternberg, 1987). We are not trying to teach students only to appreciate how psychologists think but also to become psychological thinkers themselves. Thus, we can give the students questions in class (or on exams, or in homework assignments) that require them to think triarchically. They will learn by doing far more than they will learn just by reading about how it is done.

Students also need professors to model this kind of thinking for them. As Vygotsky (1978) pointed out, students learn how to think for themselves by internalizing the thinking processes they observe in others. When we look back on our college careers and remember who our very best teachers were, we recognize that these teachers were not typically the ones who crammed content into lectures. Students who reflect back will also find that the most memorable teachers were not always the ones who were the most entertaining, even if, at the time, entertainment seemed to be of paramount importance. Rather, the outstanding teachers are often those whose thinking we most admired and incorporated into our own way of viewing the world.

Much of education is taking a little bit of one teacher's way of thinking, a little bit of another's, and a little bit of yet another's, and then combining these ways with one's own ideas in order to formulate a way of thinking that works for oneself. Modeling, therefore, is key. In effect, much of learning in college is social learning (Bandura, 1977).

How can triarchic thinking be introduced into a curriculum? Really, it's rather easy, and because instructors want all students to learn to think in all three ways, differentiation isn't necessary: Every student needs to learn to think in all three ways.

To foster analytical thinking, instructors might encourage students to compare two theories of dreaming—say, those of Freud and of Crick; or instructors might ask students to suggest how a classical experiment such as the Festinger–Carlsmith (1959) study of forced compliance could generate so many alternative interpretations; or students might be encouraged to evaluate the evidence in favor of the validity of a theory, such as the cognitive theory of depression.

To foster creative thinking, instructors might ask students to come up with their own theory of dreaming, perhaps one that selectively combines some elements of past theories with some elements of their own; to design an experiment to resolve some of the ambiguities of the Festinger–Carlsmith experiment; or to speculate on whether the cognitive theory of depression would apply equally well in a society that is more collectivist and less individualist.

To foster practical thinking, instructors might encourage students to think about the implications of a theory of dreaming for understanding a dream they have had; or the students might think about how they have used cognitive dissonance to resolve inconsistencies between their own thought and behavior; or they might reflect on how they might help a friend who is depressed, taking into account their preferred theory of depression.

The point is that exercises such as these can be injected practically anywhere into an introductory psychology course. And it is important not to save the thinking until the end of the chapter, or the end of the lecture. Why?

First, students need to understand that thinking is a part of learning—that as they think to learn, they will learn to think. Thinking is not merely something that comes after one has learned a set of concepts. Indeed, actively thinking about material as one learns it helps one to learn it (Brown & DeLoache, 1978). To the extent that students see thinking as separate from learning, they have not really understood either thinking or learning.

Second, when the "thinking" exercises are saved until the end of the chapter or lecture, thinking often just never happens. The instructor never quite gets to the end of the lecture, or the student skips the end matter in a chapter for lack of time. Unless the thinking is fully infused into the instruction, it may come to be viewed as an "extra" in which one engages as time permits (see Sternberg & Spear-Swerling, 1996).

Finally, to the extent that one views the purpose of the introductory course as one of teaching students how to think as psychologists, thinking simply cannot be separated from the course proper: It is the course proper. It is as much a part of the course as is anything else the student does.

It is crucial that assessments in the course reflect the way the course is taught. If one encourages students to think triarchically (or any other way) in class, but then uses only multiple-choice recall questions from a test bank (or anywhere else) on an exam, students will quickly learn that serious thinking is something for which they will not be held responsible. It is just an add-on to fill in a lecture or a seminar. Or if students are tested for thinking but instructed in a way that is nothing else but dry lectures wherein students are supposed merely to write down facts, then the students will again be confronted with an assessment that does not match the way in which they are being taught. Assessment and instruction must agree.

Patterns of Capitalization and Compensation

Triarchic teaching and assessment serve an important set of goals that unidimensional methods of teaching and assessment do not. This is the goal of helping students to capitalize on strengths and to compensate for and correct weaknesses.

Notions of g, or general intellectual ability, do not take into account that almost everyone is good at some things and not so good at others. Our own research (Sternberg, 1996; Sternberg, Ferrari, Clinkenbeard, & Grigorenko, 1996) has shown, for example, that the students who are strong analytically are often not those who are particularly strong creatively, that those who are strong creatively are often not those who are particularly strong practically, and that those who are strong analytically are often not those who are particularly strong practically. In fact, on my own triarchic abilities test, the correlations are generally modest among the three kinds of abilities.

To succeed in their psychology courses and in other courses as well, and later on in life, students need to learn their own individual patterns of strengths and weaknesses. They need to know where their potential contribution lies and where it doesn't. By teaching triarchically, you are practically ensuring that at least some of what you do will reach some of the students some of the time, while realizing that nothing you do will reach all of the students all of the time. Most current courses are oriented almost exclusively toward memory learners. Triarchic courses are oriented as well toward analytical, creative, and practical thinkers.

We need to teach to students' weaknesses as well as to their strengths. Why? Because students need to learn patterns of compensation for weaknesses and also how to correct their weaknesses. Abilities are modifiable (Sternberg, 1986, 1988), and by challenging students to learn in ways that are less as well as more comfortable for them, teachers help students stretch themselves. Thus, in triarchic teaching, all students get at least some instruction that matches their strengths. By teaching to students' strengths, we concretely improve the students' course performance (Sternberg & Clinkenbeard, 1995; Sternberg et al., 1996).

Other instruction needs to challenge the students to compensate for and correct weaknesses so that the students will be able to confront all of the many kinds of intellectual challenges they will encounter throughout their lives. It is not enough just to know how to do what you do well in life. You also have to know your way around or through the things you do not do so well. Such knowledge is acquired through a slow learning process.

Psychology as a Process

Too often, psychology is taught only as a product, not as a process. When I was a student in introductory psychology, the course was taught as though there was a more or less fixed knowledge base of psychology that all good students needed to know. Psychology was presented as a hard science course, with hard facts. It never really occurred to me then—and, I suspect, to most students—that the field would look very different in 10 or even 5 years.

Psychology, like all sciences, is in a constant state of flux. Today's facts are tomorrow's fictions, or more likely, tomorrow's forgottens. The answers change as the questions change, and students need to understand that all sciences begin with questions. The answers depend on the questions that have been asked.

Truly great scientists are those who ask fundamental questions—who have genuinely good taste in the problems they pursue (Zuckerman, 1977). Truly great students learn to think in terms of the questions being asked, not just in terms of the answers being given. And they learn that the questions asked in a field—whether in psychology or in another field—often proceed in a programmatic fashion, following what Hegel (1807/1931) referred to as a *dialectic*.

The basic notion of the dialectic is that someone or some group of individuals proposes a set of ideas—a thesis. Sooner or later, another individual or group of individuals proposes a contrary set of ideas—an antithesis. Eventually, a third individual or group of individuals (or, sometimes, one of the parties to the original controversy) proposes a synthesis of the opposing points of view, melding them together into a unified set of ideas. This synthesis, in turn, eventually becomes the new thesis that is attacked in a subsequent antithesis, and onward the process goes. Consider three examples of successively greater scope.

Festinger and Carlsmith (1959) accounted for what at the time seemed like a stunning result—that participants in an experiment would be more favorable toward that experiment if they were paid $1 than if they were paid $20—in terms of cognitive-dissonance theory. Some years thereafter, Bem (1967, 1972) proposed a self-perception theory explanation of these results. The two views seemed incompatible. Eventually, Fazio, Zanna, and Cooper (1977) came along and suggested that dissonance theory seems to apply better when people behave in ways that do not follow at all well from their usual beliefs or attitudes, whereas self-perception theory seems to apply better when people behave in ways that are only slightly discrepant from their normal patterns of behavior. Thesis gave way to antithesis, which gave way to a synthesis (actually, one of several).

Consider a dialectic at a larger level. Early in the twentieth century, views of the development of intellect were largely hereditarian. As anyone who has read Gould (1981) will know, the views of the early pioneers such as Goddard and Brigham, by today's standards, sound not only hereditarian, but also incredibly racist. It is hard for scholars of today to believe that professors such as these could have held positions at major universities or, perhaps, at any universities at all. By the 1960s and the 1970s, the pendulum had swung strongly in the opposite direction. Explanations of intellectual differences were very largely environmental, and behavioral geneticists had great difficulty not only being heard but also getting the funding that allowed them to do their work so that they could be heard. By the 1990s, a synthesis had been found in work such as that of Plomin (1997) and others that seriously considers how genetics and environment interact.

Finally, consider a dialectic at an even larger level. Plato and later Descartes and others proposed a paradigm and methodology for understanding the world that is largely rationalist in character. Aristotle and later Locke and others proposed a paradigm and methodology that is largely empirical. It was for Kant to figure out a way of synthesizing what previously had seemed to be incompatible methods of understanding the world—the thesis of rationalism and the antithesis of empiricism. (See Robinson, 1995, for a discussion of these contributions.) The debate, of course, continues, as does the formation of many new points of view.

Teaching Across the Curriculum

Psychology has in common with all of the social sciences as well as with the humanities its goal of trying to understand human nature. Different disciplines seek such understanding in different ways, and all have their unique as well as shared contributions to make to human understanding.

As psychologists, most of us teach only psychological points of view, although we may teach diverse psychological views that often differ among themselves as much as, say, do the perspectives of psychology and anthropology, or even of psychology and literature. Students, in contrast, typically study human behavior from many different points of view, including those of other social sciences and the humanities. Although we would like to believe that students will see the connections, they often don't. Indeed, as novices in these fields, they often have difficulty even seeing the connections within a given field.

Because learning is better when it is integrated and interconnected, students are more likely to learn material they need to learn when professors help them form these interconnections. Thus, to the extent that instructors can cite examples of psychological concepts from other fields—from literature, from art, from history, from anthropology, and so forth—the students stand to benefit in their understanding of psychology, in particular, and in their understanding of human nature, in general.

Multiculturalism and Cross-Culturalism

Terms such as *multiculturalism* and *cross-culturalism* have become such buzz words in education that it has become difficult to listen to them without thinking that they represent little more than the fad of the 1990s. They are not just a fad. These concepts are here to stay and can only increase in importance. From a societal point of view, they will increase in importance simply because American society is becoming more and more multicultural.

There is a more fundamental reason, however, for the importance of these concepts, one that applies in any culture: Without an understanding of how psychology applies multiculturally and cross-culturally, we do not really understand how psychology applies even within a single cultural context.

Consider as an example the concept of *intelligence*. Americans have a history of terribly ethnocentric views of intelligence. It turns out, however, that conceptions of intelligence differ quite widely across cultures (see, e.g., Berry, 1984; Wober, 1974), as do the kinds of tests of intelligence on which people do better or worse (see, e.g., Heath, 1983; Kearins, 1981). Understanding intelligence only as it is studied or measured in a single cultural context is a disservice to the students and to the field as well. One understands only a small and incomplete part of the story. The same is true of other psychological constructs as well, such as love, conceptions of which have varied widely over time and across cultures (see, e.g., Ackerman, 1994; Hunt, 1987; Sternberg, 1995a, in press).

In summary, to understand a construct in one sociocultural context, we need to understand how it is similar and different in other cultural contexts. If we fail to seek such understanding, we risk turning our psychology courses into unhappy opportunities for students to learn to think ethnocentrically. We have enough such thinking in the history of our field. It is time to put it behind us.

Conclusion

The goal of an introductory psychology course should be to teach students to think as psychologists. To think as psychologists, students must master the knowledge base of the field, and they need to learn to think analytically, creatively, and practically with this knowledge base. At the same time, they should be encouraged to learn their patterns of strengths and weaknesses and how to capitalize on their strengths while at the same time compensate for and correct their weaknesses. Students need to understand psychology not just as a product but also as a dialectical process and to realize that understandings of psychology vary in some (although certainly not all) respects from one culture and from one time period to another.

Not all of our introductory psychology students will become psychologists. All of them can and should learn, however, to recognize, define, and solve problems as psychologists do. These are skills we need to develop in our students and, as lifelong learners, in ourselves. I should know: I'm still trying to recognize, define, and solve the problem of that *C* in my introductory psychology course!

References

Ackerman, D. (1994). *A natural history of love*. New York: Random House.

Baddeley, A. (1986). Working memory. Oxford, England: Oxford University Press.

Bandura, A. (1977). *Social learning theory*. Englewood Cliffs, NJ: Prentice Hall.

Baron, J. B., & Sternberg, R. J. (Eds.). (1987). *Teaching thinking skills: Theory and practice*. New York: Freeman.

Bem, D. J. (1967). Self-perception: An alternative interpretation of cognitive dissonance phenomena. *Psychological Review, 74*, 183–200.

Bem, D. J. (1972). Self perception theory. In L. Berkowitz (Ed.), *Advances in experimental social psychology* (Vol. 6, pp. 1–62). San Diego, CA: Academic Press.

Berry, J. W. (1984). Towards a universal psychology of cognitive competence. In P. S. Fry (Ed.), *Changing conceptions of intelligence and intellectual functioning* (pp. 35–61). Amsterdam: North-Holland.

Brown, A. L., & DeLoache, J. S. (1978). Skills, plans, and self-regulation. In R. Siegler (Ed.), *Children's thinking: What develops?* (pp. 3–35). Hillsdale, NJ: Erlbaum.

Chi, M. T. H., Glaser, R., & Farr, M. J. (Eds.). (1988). *The nature of expertise*. Hillsdale, NJ: Erlbaum.

Chi, M. T. H., Glaser, R., & Rees, E. (1982). Expertise in problem solving. In R. J. Sternberg (Ed.), *Advances in the psychology of human intelligence* (Vol. 1, pp. 7–75). Hillsdale, NJ: Erlbaum.

Chi, M. T. H., & Koeske, R. D. (1983). Network representations of a child's dinosaur knowledge. *Developmental Psychology, 19*, 29–39.

Craik, F. I. M., & Tulving, E. (1975). Depth of processing and the retention of words in episodic memory. *Journal of Experimental Psychology: General, 104*, 268–294.

Fazio, R. H., Zanna, M. P., & Cooper, J. (1977). Dissonance and self perception: An integrative view of each theory's proper domain of application. *Journal of Experimental Social Psychology, 13*, 464–479.

Festinger, L., & Carlsmith, J. M. (1959). Cognitive consequences of forced compliance. *Journal of Abnormal and Social Psychology, 58,* 203–210.

Gould, S. J. (1981). *The mismeasure of man.* New York: Norton.

Heath, S. B. (1983). *Ways with words.* Cambridge, England: Cambridge University Press.

Hegel, G. W. F. (1931). *The phenomenology of mind* (2nd ed.; J. B. Baille, Trans.). London: Allen & Unwin. (Original work published 1807)

Hunt, M. (1987). *A natural history of love.* New York: Barnes & Noble.

Kearins, J. M. (1981). Visual spatial memory in Australian aboriginal children of desert regions. *Cognitive Psychology, 13,* 434–460.

Larkin, J., McDermott, J., Simon, D. P., & Simon, H. A. (1980). Expert and novice performance in solving physics problems. *Science, 208,* 1335–1342.

Mayer, R. E., & Greeno, J. G. (1972). Structural differences between learning outcomes produced by different instructional methods. *Journal of Educational Psychology, 63,* 165–173.

Plomin, R. (1997). Identifying genes for cognitive abilities and disabilities. In R. J. Sternberg & E. L. Grigorenko (Eds.), *Intelligence, heredity and environment* (pp. 89–104). Cambridge, England: Cambridge University Press.

Robinson, D. N. (1995). *An intellectual history of psychology* (3rd ed.). Madison: University of Wisconsin Press.

Sternberg, R. J. (1985). *Beyond IQ: A triarchic theory of human intelligence.* Cambridge, England: Cambridge University Press.

Sternberg, R. J. (1986). *Intelligence applied: Understanding and increasing your intellectual skills.* San Diego, CA: Harcourt Brace Jovanovich.

Sternberg, R. J. (1988). *The triarchic mind: A new theory of human intelligence.* New York: Viking.

Sternberg, R. J. (1994a). Diversifying instruction and assessment. *The Educational Forum, 59,* 47–53.

Sternberg, R. J. (1994b). A triarchic model for teaching and assessing students in general psychology. *General Psychologist, 30,* 42–48.

Sternberg, R. J. (1995). *In search of the human mind.* Orlando, FL: Harcourt Brace.

Sternberg, R. J. (1996) *Successful intelligence.* New York: Simon & Schuster.

Sternberg, R. J. (in press). *Love is a story.* New York: Oxford University Press.

Sternberg, R. J., & Clinkenbeard, P. (1995). A triarchic view of identifying, teaching, and assessing gifted children. *Roeper Review, 17,* 255–260.

Sternberg, R. J., Ferrari, M., Clinkenbeard, P., & Grigorenko, E. L. (1996). Identification, instruction, and assessment of gifted children: A construct validation of a triarchic model. *Gifted Child Quarterly, 40,* 129–137.

Sternberg, R. J., & Spear-Swerling, L. (1996). *Teaching for thinking.* Washington, DC: American Psychological Association.

Tulving, E. (1983). *Elements of episodic memory.* Oxford, England: Oxford University Press.

Vygotsky, L. S. (1978). *Mind in society: The development of higher psychological processes.* Cambridge, MA: Harvard University Press.

Wober, M. (1974). Towards an understanding of the Kiganda concept of intelligence. In J. W. Berry & P. R. Dasen (Eds.), *Culture and cognition: Readings in cross-cultural psychology* (pp. 261–280). London: Methuen.

Zuckerman, H. (1977). The scientific elite: Nobel Laureates' mutual influences. In R. S. Albert (Ed.), *Genius and eminence: The social psychology of creativity and exceptional achievement* (pp. 241–252). Oxford, England: Oxford University Press.

Carole E. Wade

On Thinking Critically About Introductory Psychology | 10

any years ago, when I was still a novice teacher, a student in introductory psychology complained to me about a multiple-choice item on a test, an item that had required a simple inference. "This question is not fair," groused the student. "It requires us to think." This comment got me thinking.

I knew that I had been doing my best to convey the core concepts, theories, and findings of psychology. I had been trying hard to make the course engaging and appealing: doing lots of demonstrations, inviting guest lecturers to class, even bringing a live rat to class and conditioning it to press a bar. Yet something essential was missing. At the end of each semester, as the course drew to a close, I had the depressing feeling that I was teaching merely one damned thing after another, with no glue to hold all the bits and pieces together. I was teaching content but not substance.

I began to realize that in addition to conveying the basic findings of psychology, I also needed to get my students to reflect on and use what they were learning—to show them how psychologists think and to encourage them to do the same. After all, psychology is not merely the sum of its studies; it is also a way of approaching and analyzing the world, a way of asking questions about everything from the smallest curiosities to the largest matters of life and death. Unless I could help my students acquire the thinking skills they needed to evaluate the many answers being offered to these questions, and unless they could use what they knew in reasoned discussion after leaving the class, the whole enterprise seemed pointless; to paraphrase Theodore Roszak, they would be left with data, data everywhere, but not a thought to think.

Moreover, to acquire these skills, students would have to forget some of what they already "knew" about psychology. The conventional notion about teaching anything, whether psychology, physics, or history, is that you fill students up with important facts and theories; thus the most common metaphor for learning equates the learner with a sponge, to be wrung out periodically on exams. Our discipline, of course, has plenty of important facts and theories for students to soak up. But just as an infant's nervous system matures through two processes, the acquisition of new synaptic connections and the pruning away of extraneous and counterproductive ones, so is it a student's understanding of psychology can grow only if the student acquires new knowledge and also forgets some of the junk psychology that he or she already "knows" from tabloid newspapers and TV talk shows.

Many students enter their first class in psychology "knowing," for example, that horoscopes predict the future, that they have had former lives (often as royalty, rarely as serfs), and that women are from Venus but men are from Mars. These students need a strong antidote to what R. D. Rosen (1977) called "psychobabble"—pseudoscience and quackery covered by a veneer of psychological language. In the early 1970s, when I started teaching, psychobabble was most often spoken in encounter groups designed to transform a person's rotten life in a weekend and in unconventional therapies, such as, for example, primal scream therapy, in which people are supposed to link their current unhappiness to the trauma of being born (this therapy still exists). Today, belief in the paranormal and in psychology's pseudoscientific competitors is more popular than ever; when the Central Intelligence Agency spends $20 million on psychics, we are in trouble. Unvalidated, unsupported therapies, unfortunately accepted by many mental health professionals, continue to spring up like crabgrass. A recent example is facilitated communication, which supposedly enables previously uncommunicative autistic and retarded children to type out their innermost thoughts. In fact, controlled research shows this to be facilitator communication; the children's responses are due not to their latent abilities but rather to the facilitator's unconscious hand movements. In this high-tech age, we also hear plenty of psychobabble about electronic gizmos that supposedly supercharge the brain or subliminal tapes that promise to make you happy, thin, rich, successful, healthy, and able to speak four languages, all while you sleep. Students are often attracted to such nonsense because of an intolerance for uncertainty; they want answers to their questions and solutions to their problems, and they want them now. Even some of my most capable and motivated students are sometimes attracted to simplistic pop psychology dogmas about "codependency," "women who love too much," and so on.

My thoughts on these matters eventually evolved into an approach that emphasizes critical and creative thinking: the understanding that knowledge is advanced when people resist leaping to conclusions on the basis of personal experience alone (so tempting in psychological matters), when they apply rigorous standards of evidence, and when they listen to competing views. My colleague Carol Tavris and I have since developed a systematic approach to critical thinking that emphasizes not only the skills that it requires but also the disposition to use those skills. *Critical thinking*, which we define as the ability and willingness to assess claims and make judgments on the basis of well-supported reasons, serves as the guiding philosophy both in our teaching and in our textbooks. Our goal is to involve students actively in the evaluation of what they read and hear and to get them to appreciate the unfinished, open-ended nature of intellectual inquiry. In short, we want them to think.

Our approach, however, is not equivalent to mere debunking. All too often, critical thought is equated with an extreme philosophical skepticism, the notion that nothing is ever really known. Those who take this approach often focus solely on getting students to spot fallacies in arguments. We prefer a gentler, more pragmatic sort of skepticism, which demands that evidence be used to support conclusions but that also includes a positive search for explanations. The "just say no" message in some approaches to critical thinking, we believe, is likely to lead students to a radical relativism—the belief that because any position is vulnerable to attack, one judgment or interpretation is as good as any other.

Undergraduate students are especially vulnerable to radical relativism, for as Patricia King and Karen Kitchener have shown in their studies of reflective judgment (King & Kitchener, 1994; Kitchener & King, 1981, 1990), most students think in only a quasi-reflective manner and tend to doubt that anything can be known rationally. They recognize that some things cannot be known with absolute certainty, but they are not sure how to deal with these situations. They realize that judgments should be supported by reasons, but they pay attention only to evidence that fits what they already believe. They know that there are alternative viewpoints, but they seem to think that because knowledge is uncertain, any judgment about the evidence is purely subjective. They will justify their beliefs by what "feels right"; they will tell you that everything is "relative" and that "everyone has a right to their own opinion," as if all opinions were created equal. Kitchener and King found that even at age 22 to 25, many people see reality as a matter of interpretation and say that knowledge is entirely subjective. Only later, at an older age than that of the traditional undergraduate and after considerable education, are they likely to recognize that although reality is never a "given" and although claims may remain open to reevaluation, it is nonetheless possible to say that some judgments or interpretations of ill-structured problems are more valid than others. It follows from this research that those of us who wish to help students think more critically must recognize that the epistemological assumptions they bring to the classroom may differ considerably from our own.

On the bright side, when students get support for thinking reflectively and opportunities for practice, their thinking tends to become more complex, sophisticated, and well grounded (Kitchener, Lynch, Fischer, & Wood, 1993). There are, of course, many approaches to teaching critical thinking (e.g., Halpern, 1995; Levy, 1997; Paul, 1984; Ruggiero, 1988). After studying the literature, we condensed the various skills and dispositions discussed by other writers to eight basic guidelines:

1. Ask questions: be willing to wonder. To think critically about psychology, one must by willing to think creatively—to be curious about the puzzles of human behavior, to wonder why people act the way they do, and to question received explanations and examine new ones.

2. Define the problem. Once a question has been raised, the next step is to identify the issues involved in clear and concrete terms, rather than vague ones such as "happiness," "potential," or "meaningfulness." The inadequate formulation of a question can produce misleading or incomplete answers. For example, the question "Can animals learn language?" assumes that language is an all-or-none ability, and it allows for only two possible answers, yes or no. Putting the question another way—"Which aspects of language might certain animals be able to acquire?"—takes into account that language requires many different abilities. It also acknowledges the differences among species and opens up a range of possible answers.

3. Examine the evidence. A critical thinker considers the nature of the evidence supporting various approaches to the problem under examination. Is it reliable? Valid? Is the "evidence" merely someone's personal assertion or speculation? If the evidence is scientific in nature, does it come from one or two narrow studies or from repeated research? If it is not possible to check the reliability of the evidence, the critical thinker considers whether the source has been reliable in the past.

4. Analyze biases and assumptions. Critical thinkers evaluate the assumptions and biases that lie behind arguments, asking how they influence claims and conclusions. They consider any prejudices or deeply held values that might affect the evaluation of a problem. They are willing to consider evidence that contradicts their own beliefs and to examine the biases of others.

5. Avoid emotional reasoning ("If I feel this way, it must be true"). Emotion has a place in psychological science: Passionate commitment to a view can motivate a person to think boldly without fear of what others will say, to defend an unpopular idea, and to seek evidence for creative new theories. Moreover, everyone holds convictions and ideas about how the world should operate; life would be impossible without them. However, people with opposing views on an issue are often equally serious and sincere about their convictions, so feelings cannot substitute for careful appraisal of arguments and evidence.

6. Do not oversimplify. Critical thinking requires a person to look beyond the obvious, watch out for logical contradictions, be wary of argument by anecdote, and, most important, avoid either–or thinking. For example, is it better in terms of physical and mental health to feel a sense of control over events or to accept with tranquillity whatever life serves up? Either answer oversimplifies. A sense of control has many benefits; for example, it helps to reduce pain, improve adjustment to surgery and illness, and speed up recovery from some diseases (Ewart, 1995). Sometimes, however, it is best to "go with the flow"; people who have the unrealistic belief that they can control everything about their disease often do not adjust well to it (Thompson, Nanni, & Levine, 1994).

7. Consider other interpretations. Before leaping to a conclusion, the critical thinker examines other hypotheses that offer reasonable explanations of characteristics, behavior, and events. The ultimate goal is to find an explanation that accounts for the most evidence with the fewest assumptions. The critical thinker is especially careful about drawing premature conclusions about cause and effect.

8. Tolerate uncertainty. This may be the hardest step in becoming a critical thinker. Sometimes there is not enough evidence available to warrant any conclusion, and sometimes the evidence allows only a tentative conclusion. Although we all need some guiding ideas and beliefs, this guideline requires a willingness to give them up when new information calls them into question.

Tavris and I do not view critical thinking as a gimmick to be tacked onto the text as a special feature or discussed once in a lecture and then never mentioned again. It cannot be summed up in a short phrase or mnemonic (such as, say, SQ3R) or in a set of rhetorical questions, because it is a theme woven throughout the course, one that encourages students, at every possible opportunity, to examine the significance of what they are learning and to temper open-mindedness with intellectual caution and humility.

Of course, to think critically, one must have something to think about. We believe that this "something" must include the controversies that stimulate lively, and sometimes angry, debate in our discipline. These controversies make psychology fascinating, and students should not be sheltered from them. They should know, for example, that evolutionary psychologists and feminist psychologists often differ strongly in their analyses of gender relations. They should know that psychodynamic clinicians and experimental psychologists differ strongly in their assumptions about memory, child development, and trauma and that these differences have profound implications in the debates over "recovered memory" and the questioning of children as eyewitnesses. They should know that the "scientist–practitioner gap" threatens to become a chasm, and why that is so. In our teaching and writing, therefore, we candidly address these and other issues, trying to show why they occur, and we suggest the kinds of questions that might lead to useful answers in each case.

Now, if a teacher (or writer) wants to emphasize important debates and how to think about them—if the course is to be something other than an extended *Psychology Review* article—then something has to go; as every teacher of the introductory course knows only too well, there is only so much time available. Much of what gets taught in the introductory course is there because of tradition, and some of it is covered in the kind of detail that we think ought to be left for more advanced courses. Our approach, therefore, demands that every study or topic included justify inclusion. Our guiding question is, What should an educated citizen know about psychology?

Eliminating some detail does *not* mean "watering down" the course. Far from it: We believe that our strategy for teaching adds complexity, by making room for the conceptual problems and issues that psychologists argue about so passionately in their journals and at professional meetings, and for the questions that drive psychological researchers into their laboratories in the middle of the night. It is a serious mistake, in our opinion, to equate *level* with *detail*, for the mind thinks with ideas as well as information. An encyclopedic course will inevitably sacrifice depth and thoughtfulness, in the rush to cram an overwhelming amount of material into 10 or 15 weeks. A "just the basics" approach, on the other hand, often does not introduce important technical terms and may not encourage thinking because it short-changes research methods and important disagreements in the field. A course that emphasizes substance over minutia, however, has conceptual sophistication without being overwhelming. If it succeeds, it cannot easily be pegged as high level or low level, because the dichotomy itself is false.

At the risk of alienating some readers, let me give an example. Many teachers and textbooks go into great detail about the molecular chemistry of the neural impulse, including information about sodium and potassium pumps and ion channels. In my experience teaching at both 2-year and 4-year colleges, most students come into the introductory course with only a hazy idea of what a neuron is, and most do not have a clue about what neurotransmitters do. More important, they do not yet have the intellectual tools to evaluate claims about the biochemical basis of mental disorders or the use of drugs in treatment. If they were depressed and a physician recommended medication, they would not know how to think critically about the efficacy and long-term risks of the proposed treatment. They are unaware of the pitfalls of biological reductionism, and they have not learned that brain abnormalities that show up in brain-scan studies of people with psychological disorders do not necessarily clarify the relationship between cause and effect. We therefore emphasize these important problems rather than the biochemical details of neural transmission. If the student learns the intricacies of the action potential but cannot spot the dangers of biological reductionism when reading accounts of findings in the newspaper, or cannot assess someone's claim to have found "the" gene for aggression, how knowledgeable is that student about the biological bases of behavior?

Here is another example. How can teachers introduce a student to the fundamental topics and approaches of cognitive psychology, when only 1 week (at most) is devoted to thinking and another to memory? Again, this challenge requires some critical thinking about which findings are truly appropriate for the introductory course. In our teaching and our textbooks, therefore, we have chosen to leave out some details about concept formation, but to require students to know about such important cognitive biases (and barriers to critical thinking) as the confirmation bias (Kuhn, Weinstock, & Flaton, 1994; Kunda, 1990) and the hindsight bias (Fischhoff, 1975; Hawkins & Hastie, 1990). Similarly, in our coverage of heritability, we do not cover all the technicalities of the structure of DNA, but we do expect students to understand why estimates of heritability apply only to groups of people and not to individuals; that *heritable* does not mean the same thing as *genetic;*

and that heritability estimates apply only to a particular group living in a particular environment.

Of course, it is important for students in the introductory course to learn the classic studies in the field—Milgram's obedience studies, Skinner's operant-conditioning studies, Sherif's studies on cooperation and competition. However, it is equally important that they learn to recognize the difference between a strong study and a weak one. Those who go on in psychology will meet the classic studies again, in subsequent courses. Those who do not may forget the details of many studies, but they will continue to come across new findings for the rest of their lives—in newspapers and magazines and on television—and they will need the skills to assess these findings wisely. Both majors and nonmajors, therefore, must have an understanding of the kinds of questions psychologists ask, the methods they use, and the assumptions those in the various subfields make, as well as the major findings in the discipline.

It is our belief that an emphasis on issues, controversies, and the thoughtful evaluation of information actually provides students with the cognitive scaffolding necessary for long-term retention of the factual material they must learn. As cognitive psychologists have long known, learning a bunch of disconnected facts is hard, and people tend to remember better when they have some coherent cognitive schemas into which they can fit the discrete pieces of information they must learn. As anyone who has given a comprehensive final knows, when these schemas are lacking, students may not even retain all that they have learned until the end of the semester.

What about retention of discrete facts for the longer term? Studies of this issue have been surprisingly rare, but the few that have been published are not encouraging. For example, 4 months after the end of the semester, Rickard, Rogers, Ellis, and Beidleman (1988) gave a multiple-choice test of general psychology content to students who had taken introductory psychology but were not enrolled in a second psychology course, and they compared the students' performance with that of students who had never taken a psychology course and who had comparable college grade point averages. Although the psychology students did better and the differences were statistically significant, the advantage shown by the instructed students was small in practical terms. In another study (Gustav, 1969), an objective test covering introductory material was given on a surprise basis to 343 students in advanced psychology courses; only half the students passed. Moreover, scores showed only a slight positive correlation with reported final grades and with the amount of time that had elapsed since taking the introductory course. Although high school psychology courses often do not have the scientific focus that college courses do, it is also interesting that several studies find no relationship whatsoever between having completed a high school course and performance in an introductory college course (e.g., Griggs & Jackson, 1988; Hedges & Thomas, 1980).

Students who go on to more advanced courses do eventually retain a great deal of what they have learned, especially if the material can be represented schematically (see Conway, Cohen, & Stanhope, 1992); otherwise, no one would pass the Graduate Record Exam. Most students in the introductory course, however, are not psychology majors, and the course is not only the first but also the last opportunity they have to study the findings and methods of our discipline in an organized, systematic way. Faced with 10 zillion studies and 3 thousand theories and only one semester (usually) to teach them, teachers and textbook authors must be selective.

Inevitably, an emphasis on critical inquiry requires attention to issues of culture, ethnicity, and gender. One cannot think critically about psychology without noticing that there is something scientifically wrong about trying to deduce universal principles of behavior from a narrow sample of humanity—Americans, say, or White college sophomores, or middle-class men. From the start, our approach has to "mainstream" culture, ethnicity, and gender by raising relevant studies throughout the text.

Again, however, it does little good to cover findings unless students also learn how to grapple with the difficult controversies raised by the findings. In some books and many classrooms, for example, multiculturalism seems neither "multi" nor "cultural," but rather a pretext for celebrating diverse ethnic identities. There is a place for such celebration, but students also need to understand what culture means, why there are often tensions within and among ethnic minority groups, and how culture affects conceptions of time, interdependence, and the self. They need to think about why the subject of "political correctness" in group names is such an emotional one, why the study of culture so often deteriorates into stereotyping and value judgments, and why prejudice comes in different forms and degrees. They need to ask why cultures change over time, and why cultural traditions often persist even when they cause hardship and suffering. Most of all, they need to be exposed to the scientific study of culture— to problems of definition, method, and interpretation, along with some of the excellent research now available.

Because we emphasize issues, controversies, and organizing narratives that make discrete findings understandable and meaningful, we do not simply end the course (or our textbooks) with the last topic (say, social psychology). Instead, the course culminates in a capstone assignment that has the student integrate, apply, and evaluate the diverse findings as well as the psychological perspectives that have been covered: biological, learning, cognitive, sociocultural, and psychodynamic. The student selects a real-life issue for analysis, either a personal issue, such as a problem in a relationship or difficulties in studying, or a social or political issue, such as homelessness or recidivism among prisoners. In one version of the assignment, the student focuses on any five relevant findings or theories from the course, describes them in some detail, and shows how they might illuminate or help resolve the problem at hand. In another version, the student describes and applies the five major psychological perspectives. With either version, students gain practice in thinking independently, drawing connections between concepts and findings, and seeing the relevance of what they have learned to problems that have no single, easy answer. Usually students complete this exercise with an understanding that no one finding or approach to psychology is adequate for solving the fuzzy problems of real life.

The philosophy of teaching that I have described is consistent with recommendations that emerged several years ago from the American Association for the Advancement of Science's (AAAS) Project 2061, an effort to determine how best to increase scientific literacy. The AAAS commissioned the National Council on Science and Technology Education to survey hundreds of scientists, engineers, and educators and draw up a report of their recommendations. The result, *Science for All Americans*, calls on instructors to "reduce the sheer amount of material covered"; to "present the scientific endeavor as a social enterprise that strongly influences—and is influenced by—human thought and action"; and to "foster scientific ways of thinking" (AAAS Project 2061, 1989; for the report from the social and behavioral sciences panel, see Appley & Maher, 1989).

Psychology as a discipline has grown by leaps and bounds since most of us took our first introductory course. Students today often feel that they are drowning in a sea of information. A critical thinking approach offers them a lifeboat that not only keeps them afloat but also enables them to steam ahead in the turbulent, mysterious seas of psychology.

References

AAAS Project 2061. (1989). *Science for all Americans.* (Available from the American Association for the Advancement of Science, 1333 H Street, NW, Washington, DC 20005)

Appley, M., & Maher, W. (1989). *Science and behavior sciences: Report of the Project 2061 Phase I social and behavioral sciences panel.* (Available from the American Association for the Advancement of Science, 1333 H Street, NW, Washington, DC 20005)

Conway, M. A., Cohen, G., & Stanhope, M. (1992). Very long-term memory for knowledge acquired at school and university. *Applied Cognitive Psychology, 6*, 467–482.

Ewart, C. K. (1995). Self-efficacy and recovery from heart attack. In J. E. Maddux (Ed.), *Self-efficacy, adaptation, and adjustment: Theory, research, and application.* New York: Plenum.

Fischhoff, B. (1975). Hindsight is not equal to foresight: The effect of outcome knowledge on judgment under uncertainty. *Journal of Experimental Psychology: Human Perception and Performance, 1*, 288–299.

Griggs, R. A., & Jackson, S. L. (1988). A reexamination of the relationship of high school psychology and natural science courses to performance in a college introductory psychology class. *Teaching of Psychology, 15*, 142–144.

Gustav, A. (1969). Retention of course material after varying intervals of time. *Psychological Reports, 25*, 727–730.

Halpern, D. (1995). *Thought and knowledge: An introduction to critical thinking* (3rd ed.). Hillsdale, NJ: Erlbaum.

Hawkins, S. A., & Hastie, R. (1990). Hindsight: Biased judgments of past events after the outcomes are known. *Psychological Bulletin, 107*, 311–327.

Hedges, B. W., & Thomas, J. H. (1980). The effect of high school psychology on pre-course knowledge, midterm grades, and final grades in introductory psychology. *Teaching of Psychology, 7*, 221–223.

King, P. M. & Kitchener, K. S. (1994). *Developing reflective judgment: Understanding and promoting intellectual growth and critical thinking in adolescents and adults.* San Francisco: Jossey-Bass.

Kitchener, K. S., & King, P. M. (1981). Reflective judgment: Concepts of justification and their relationship to age and education. *Journal of Applied Developmental Psychology, 2*, 89–116.

Kitchener, K. S., & King, P. M. (1990). The reflective judgment model: Ten years of research. In M. L. Commons (Ed.), *Models and methods in the study of adolescent and adult thought: Vol. 2. Adult development* (pp. 63–78). Westport, CT: Greenwood.

Kitchener, K. S., Lynch, C. L., Fischer, K. W., & Wood, P. K. (1993). Developmental range of reflective judgment: The effect of contextual support and practice on developmental stage. *Developmental Psychology, 29*, 893–906.

Kuhn, D., Weinstock, M., & Flaton, R. (1994). How well do jurors reason? Competence dimensions of individual variation in a juror reasoning task. *Psychological Science, 5*, 289–296.

Kunda, Z. (1990). The case for motivated reasoning. *Psychological Bulletin, 108*, 480–498.

Levy, D. A. (1997). *Tools of critical thinking: Metathoughts for psychology.* Boston: Allyn & Bacon.

Paul, R. W. (1984, September). Critical thinking: Fundamental to education for a free society. *Educational Leadership,* 4–14.

Rickard, H. C., Rogers, R., Ellis, N. R., & Beidleman, W. B. (1988). Some retention but not enough. *Teaching of Psychology, 15,* 151–152.

Rosen, R. D. (1977). *Psychobabble.* New York: Atheneum.

Ruggiero, V. R. (1988). *Teaching thinking across the curriculum.* New York: Harper & Row.

Thompson, S. C., Nanni, C., & Levine, A. (1994). Primary versus secondary and central versus consequence-related control in HIV-positive men. *Journal of Personality and Social Psychology, 67,* 540–547.

Camille B. Wortman and Joshua M. Smyth

Using One's Own Passion and Undergraduate TAs to Transform the Large-Lecture Introductory Psychology Course

11

My first experience teaching introductory psychology occurred nearly 25 years ago. I was a new faculty member at Northwestern University, and I was asked to teach the introductory course during the winter quarter. I was told that the enrollment would be between 300 and 500 students and that I would have one graduate student teaching assistant (TA). I had virtually no teaching experience while in graduate school. During the fall term, I had struggled with an 80-person introductory social psychology course and was barely able to keep my head above water. The prospect of coming up with an entirely new set of lectures and study materials for the introductory course was daunting. I knew that I was supposed to be getting my research program off the ground, but the teaching was so all-consuming that there was little time for anything else.

The Northwestern approach to covering introductory psychology—having a teacher with a microphone confront several hundred students in a lecture hall—is the norm at most schools. Indeed, because of enrollment pressures and constrained resources, it is hard for departments to offer this course any other way. Although I understood the reasons for this pedagogical approach, I nonetheless felt strait-jacketed by it. I guess this was because I hoped to accomplish more through my teaching than conveying factual

This chapter represents an active collaboration between Camille B. Wortman and Joshua M. Smyth. Because much of it draws heavily on the personal experiences of Camille B. Wortman, however, sections are written in the first person.

163

material to the students. I wanted to spark students' intellectual curiosity about human behavior and to foster an increased understanding and tolerance of their own behavior and that of others. Mostly, I wanted students to have the opportunity to become actively engaged with the course material and to apply this material to their own life concerns.

The question facing me as I contemplated teaching my first introductory psychology course is one that I have confronted many times since: How can I teach a lively and engaging course within the constraints imposed by the large lecture format, and how can I do so in a way that permits time for activities other than teaching, such as research and having a life? In attempting to answer this question, I have tried many approaches over the years. This chapter describes two strategies that have been highly successful and that have stood the test of time. The first of these—teaching what you are passionate about—enhances the likelihood that the lectures offered in the course will be vital and engaging to the students.

Our Twofold Strategy

In this section we raise questions faced by every teacher of the introductory course: How should the lecture time be used? What topics are most important to cover? Is it really necessary to provide broad coverage of psychology in one's lectures? We argue that it is not only unnecessary to do so but also counterproductive. By focusing their lectures on topics that they know and care about, instructors can enhance interest and motivation for themselves and ultimately for their students. This approach can make material come alive through the use of personal insight, anecdotal information, and genuine interest on the part of the lecturer. We maintain that this inevitably results in lectures that are more dynamic and compelling for the students.

The second strategy—the use of undergraduate TAs—enables the instructor to change the class structure in ways that encourage student involvement and participation. Undergraduate assistants provide the opportunity for discussion of course material in a more individualized and personal fashion, allow for feedback on and evaluation of students' efforts (e.g., essays and short papers), and provide the unique opportunity to offer specialized "minicourses" (described later) on a variety of topics of particular interest and relevance to students. Both of these strategies can help make the introductory course a more engaging, active, and personal experience for the students taking it. And each can free up the instructor's time to focus on research or nonacademic interests. Below, these strategies are discussed in more detail.

Lecturing on What You Are Passionate About

An issue that all introductory psychology teachers must confront is how best to use the lecture time. Many instructors take it as a given that each week they should focus their lectures on the topics covered in the text, such as the brain, sensation and perception, learning and conditioning, cognition and language, and development. When an instructor is facing the introductory course for the first time, the idea of developing new lectures each week on these topics can seem overwhelming. Being a social psychologist, I knew next to nothing about most of these topics, and I had no idea how to make them come alive for the student. I was also concerned that if I drew my lecture material from the textbook, there would be too much redundancy between the lectures and the reading. On the other hand, if I drew my lectures from other sources, I was concerned that discrepancies could arise between the descriptions of psychological processes provided in the lectures and those in the text. Given my lack of knowledge about topics outside my area, I had no confidence that I could adequately address students' questions regarding such discrepancies.

The primary reason for my reluctance to offer lectures on the major topics covered in psychology textbooks is that this is how the introductory psychology course was taught when I was a student. Each lecture consisted of a dull recitation of facts, studies, and results relevant to a major theme in psychology such as learning or development. The course was a dreadful bore.

I was concerned that by trying to pay lip service to all of the major areas of psychology in my lectures, I would not do justice to any of them. Even the most conservative teachers of introductory psychology would probably agree that students do not benefit from attempts to provide encyclopedic coverage of our discipline. Typically, the instructor who strives for broad coverage of all the important concepts has no choice but to sacrifice depth. As one writer has indicated, it may not be possible to be encyclopedic and also be thought provoking and interesting (Candland, 1982). In recognition of the disadvantages of broad, encyclopedic coverage, many introductory psychology texts now include a section in each chapter that focuses on a specific issue in some depth.

In working out how I would use my lecture time, I went back to my goals for teaching the introductory psychology course. Of course, one of my goals was to provide coverage of the theories and data in the major subfields of psychology. But I had other goals that were closer to my heart, such as sharing information with students that could have profound relevance to their lives. I have always had a passionate desire to show students that the science of psychology has much to offer regarding such day-to-day matters as understanding one's own behavior; maintaining relationships with friends; and making decisions regarding dating, alcohol, and sex.

I knew, at some level, that if I was not lecturing about something that was vital and involving for me, the lectures would not have high interest value for the students. At that point, I decided that I would not try to cover the entire field of psychology in my lectures. I reasoned that this was why I had assigned a textbook. I began to see my job in the lectures as that of supplementing the textbook by covering topics that I wholeheartedly believed the students should know about.

When I teach introductory psychology, I select a lecture topic each week that is related to the material covered in the textbook but that does not duplicate that material. In each case, the topic is one that I have a passionate interest in conveying to the students. Let me provide some examples. In the early 1980s, my best friend and closest colleague committed suicide. This friend had made many suicide threats, and although I tried to be supportive, I had no idea what type of response would be most helpful. I still believe that if I had known more about suicide, I might have been able to do something before it was too late. For this reason, I am very interested in teaching students about suicide. I cover myths about suicide, indications of suicidal behavior, and what to say (and what not to say) to someone who is suicidal (see Hubbard & McIntosh, 1992, for additional suggestions on teaching about suicide). A related topic that I usually try to cover in my lectures is depression. Having witnessed the ravages of depression firsthand, I am extremely motivated to ensure that students understand the symptoms of this fairly common disorder and know about the treatments most effective in alleviating it. These topics are usually covered in the part of the course concerned with abnormal behavior and treatment.

Other topics that I am passionate about teaching are romantic love, violence in society (including violence against women and date rape), and drunk-driving behavior. I usually cover love and violence in the social psychology section of the course; drunk driving can be covered in the section on alcohol and drug use. In focusing on drunk driving, my goal is to challenge students' feelings of invulnerability and to dispel erroneous beliefs they may hold about drinking and driving. For example, most students believe that it is the problem drinkers who cause most of the fatalities, but in fact, the vast majority of such crashes are caused by those who drink just a little too much. I show a short film illustrating how driving performance is impaired after one, two, and three drinks. I also arrange for a panel discussion in which a quadriplegic injured in an alcohol-related crash and a mother who lost a child in a drunk-driving crash address the class and answer questions.

Another topic that I am passionate about teaching is how people cope with major life events. For the past 20 years, I have been involved in research on some of life's traumas, including cancer, rape, serious injury, and loss of a loved one. At some point, most students will experience a trauma of major proportions—a trauma for which they are ill prepared and which has the potential to change their lives forever. In fact, the evidence suggests that many of the students facing us in the classroom have already endured a significant trauma. Two students in five have grown up in homes with divorced parents, and 40% of these individuals suffer serious psychological problems as a result (Wallerstein, 1987). In one study involving a national sample of college students, over half of the women had experienced some sort of sexual victimization, ranging from unwanted fondling to rape (Koss, Gidycz, & Wisniewski, 1987). A surprisingly high percentage of students have been subjected to physical or sexual abuse by a parent or relative (Silver, Boon, & Stones, 1983). In addition to trying to deal with their own traumas, most students will encounter roommates, coworkers, friends, and family members who have experienced these and other traumas and who may turn to them for advice or support.

Why is it so important to teach students about coping with life's traumas? Most people who experience trauma do not seek professional help. Instead, they attempt to deal with the event alone or with the help of friends. Unfortunately, available evidence suggests that people hold erroneous beliefs about the process of coming to terms with a traumatic event. I believe that these beliefs can make it difficult for people to handle their own distress and also to intervene effectively with others who have experienced a trauma (for a more detailed discussion of these erroneous beliefs or myths of coping with stressful life experiences, see Wortman & Silver, 1989).

Specifically, it is widely believed that people react to traumatic events with extreme distress, that a failure to show distress is indicative of pathology, and that people should recover from a trauma within several months or a year. Although these ideas are regarded to be true by the general public and by health care professionals, there is little evidence to support them. In fact, accumulating evidence suggests that initial reactions to a stressful life experience are highly variable, with some people showing intense distress while others do not;

that failure to show distress is not necessarily indicative of pathology and may signal coping strength; and that it often takes far longer than a year to recover from the effects of a traumatic loss.

Individuals who hold these beliefs may judge their own behavior harshly if they experience a traumatic event. For example, a victim of rape or sexual abuse may infer that there is something wrong if he or she continues to experience symptoms several years after the assault. Similarly, people who hold these beliefs may react judgmentally to others. If someone manifests distress longer than a potential helper expects, that helper may convey that the person is not trying hard enough to recover. Erroneous beliefs about the process of coping with trauma can lead others to respond in a variety of ways that have been found to be unhelpful. These include discouraging expression of feelings (e.g., "tears won't bring him back"), minimizing the loss ("you had many good years together"), and offering advice ("you should consider getting a dog—they're wonderful companions"). (For a more detailed discussion of helpful and unhelpful responses to the bereaved, see Lehman, Ellard, & Wortman, 1986.)

I hope that by incorporating this information into my introductory psychology lectures, I can accomplish a number of important goals. One is to normalize people's emotional reactions to traumas that they may have experienced in the past or that they may experience in the future. By illustrating the variety of ways people respond to traumatic events, I hope to encourage students to be less judgmental toward themselves should they experience a trauma and more accepting and less critical of others who may not react as they expect. I also try to elucidate how current reactions to situations or people can be influenced by earlier traumas. For example, children from divorced families often show no difficulties in coping with their parents' divorce until they begin dating. At this point it is common to experience intense anxiety about forming intimate relationships with members of the opposite sex (Wallerstein, 1991).

One of the most important reasons to lecture on topics that one is passionate about is that when a teacher conveys enthusiasm and interest for a subject, interest is far more likely to be evoked in the students. As McKeachie (1987) noted in an article on effective teaching, the most important characteristics of effective teachers are the interest, enjoyment, and motivation they bring to the classroom. An added advantage is that in most respects, it is far easier to lecture about things we know and care about. A risk of this kind of teaching is that the more passionate one is about a given topic, the greater the danger of losing one's objectivity. When lecturing about violence, for example, I have had to use extreme self-control to avoid getting into shouting matches with students who believe it is reasonable to carry a gun. I have to remind myself that what I am really passionate about is bringing scientific evidence in psychology to bear on an important life issue, not persuading students to behave in particular ways.

When the lecture touches on such topics as suicide, rape, divorce, incest, and the death of a loved one, powerful feelings are likely to be evoked in some students. In many cases, students who have been struggling on their own with a personal problem related to these topics will become motivated to seek help. This will undoubtedly result in some difficult situations for the instructor. During office hours in a single day, I can recall talking with one student whose brother was a drug addict and one student whose parents were both dying of AIDS. That same term, I was also visited by a student who recognized, during a lecture on date rape, that he was a rapist. A danger is that when confronted with problems of this sort, the instructor will be drawn in too deeply and try to function as a psychotherapist or even a substitute parent. It is important to remember that our role is not to resolve these problems but to assist the student in obtaining help from a person who is well qualified to provide it. In our judgment, instructors should not even attempt to teach about such topics unless they are knowledgeable about how and where to make a referral. It is critically important that professors have information about referrals available before they incorporate these topics into their teaching.

Involving Undergraduates as Teaching Assistants in Introductory Psychology

The first time I decided to use undergraduate TAs, the decision was made more out of desperation than out of any sense that it would be particularly successful. I knew I did not want a large-course, lecture-only format, and there was obviously no way that a lone graduate student and I could divide up several hundred students for discussion sections. Apparently I am not the only one who recoils at the idea of facing a large, anonymous body of students each day in the introductory course. In one survey of how introductory psychology courses are staffed in departments with graduate programs, it was found that virtually all schools teach the introductory course in a large, lecture-only format (Griggs, Lange, & Meyer, 1988). Almost half of the schools surveyed reported serious problems in staffing this course.

Many schools indicated that they found it difficult to persuade faculty, especially senior faculty, to teach the introductory course under these conditions.

I made the decision to use undergraduate TAs because I saw it as a way to alter the lecture-only format and incorporate opportunities for discussion. There is considerable evidence to suggest that whereas lectures and discussions are equally effective in imparting factual knowledge, discussion sections are far superior in fostering long-term retention of factual material, critical thinking skills, and motivation for further learning (see McKeachie, 1986, for a review). Moreover, I thought that a format with regular discussion sections would enable me to structure the course so as to incorporate those topics that typically draw students to psychology classes in the first place. These include their need to do well as students (e.g., memory and study skills), to relate to other people (e. g., conflict resolution and interpersonal relationships), and to understand themselves (e.g., sexual behavior and binge eating). (See Zanich & Grover, 1989, for a survey of student interest in various topics within psychology.) Although these topics can be covered in lecture, they lend themselves particularly well to a small-group discussion format.

Another advantage of using undergraduate TAs is that it makes it possible to structure the course so as to provide different options to different students. There is abundant evidence that students taking introductory psychology have very diverse goals. In most such courses, typically more than 75% of students are not psychology majors. Hence, a course that is simply a foundation for later academic work in psychology will not meet the needs of most students. Consequently, I wanted to design the course so that nonmajors as well as majors could explore topics that were meaningful to them. A journalism major may be particularly interested in persuasion and attitude change; a speech major might wish to have some exposure to psycholinguistics. Ideally, a course structure should be flexible enough to permit this type of exploration. Most students do not typically have the opportunity to explore such interests in subsequent courses because more often than not the introductory course is the only psychology course they ever take.

Many articles about the use of undergraduate TAs appeared in the literature in the 1970s and early 1980s (e.g., Diamond, 1972; Maas & Pressler, 1973). As we detail below, these articles provide compelling evidence that the use of undergraduate assistants can play an important role in solving the problems associated with a large lecture format. Yet despite the apparent success of this approach, it has not, to our knowledge, been widely applied. Indeed, a computer search failed to reveal a single article discussing this approach that was published within the last 10 years.

As pressures intensify on college administrators to increase class size and as resources become more scarce, it may be worthwhile to consider this novel approach to teaching introductory psychology once again. It is usually feasible to recruit advanced undergraduates to assist with introductory psychology in exchange for some (typically ungraded) course credit. In schools or situations where instructors cannot give credit, having this experience to add to a resumé or graduate school application, as well as being able to request a letter of recommendation from the sponsoring faculty, is often incentive enough. A major advantage of choosing undergraduate TAs is that they are typically enthusiastic about having the opportunity to become involved in teaching. This is not always the case with graduate student TAs, who often regard teaching duties as a burden and a distraction from their research.

There are at least three different ways that advanced undergraduates can be used to help individualize a large lecture course. First, they can be involved as leaders of discussion sections much the same way as one would typically involve graduate students. Second, they can assist in providing feedback, making it possible to use forms of evaluation that are otherwise not feasible in a large lecture course, such as essay exams, short papers, and journals. Finally, undergraduate students can develop and teach specialized minicourses, or seminars on topics of high student interest, that run for 1 or 2 weeks during the term (for a more detailed discussion, see Wortman & Hillis, 1976). Through the minicourses, it is possible to offer students choice among various topics in psychology. Below, we offer more detailed information about student-led discussions, grading by undergraduate students, and student-led minicourse seminars.

DISCUSSION GROUPS

Undergraduate TAs can lead weekly discussion groups of 10–15 students. As was noted earlier, research suggests that students benefit from the active participation that such small discussion groups permit. In my introductory psychology classes, I typically have undergraduates lead discussions of paperback books, such as *Walden 2, Ordinary People,* or *Sybil,* and films, such as Milgram's film *Obedience.* Each TA is asked to write one or two discussion questions on each book, and these are compiled and shared among the TAs (I circulate discussion questions on the films). I have also asked undergraduate TAs to lead discussions focused on specific problems, such as mental illness or date rape. In so doing, I encourage them to bring in guest speakers from the community. For example, a student might invite a former mental patient to discuss mental illness or a volunteer at a rape crisis center to discuss how misattributions about another person's motives can lead to date rape. On occasion, I have asked undergraduates to use their discussion sessions to review the lectures or textbook in preparation for an upcoming test. However, I have found this to be less effective than the other options described earlier.

To enhance the value of the experience for the TA as well as the introductory psychology students, I distribute materials designed to help assistants augment their skills as discussion leaders. One useful reference is chapter 4 of McKeachie's (1986) book *Teaching Tips*. This chapter provides a wealth of information that is helpful to discussion leaders, such as how to start the discussion, how to facilitate group problem solving, how to handle nonparticipants, how to deal with students who monopolize the discussion, and what to do if students do not read the assignment and are thus unprepared to participate in the discussion.

EVALUATIVE FEEDBACK

Surveys have indicated that in the vast majority of cases, introductory psychology professors rely solely on objective tests (Ross, Anderson, & Gaulton, 1987). Use of undergraduate TAs provides the option of incorporating short-answer exams and papers into the class. We have asked undergraduate students to grade essay exams and short papers as part of their duties. Initially, I was reluctant to ask undergraduates to become involved in such grading, but evaluations have suggested that undergraduates enjoy grading as long as the amount is reasonable. It is very important to provide students with clear guidelines about how many points should be given for various kinds of answers and that the introductory students understand that such criteria are in use. Available research suggests that it is indeed possible for such grading to be done with a high degree of reliability (Bernstein, 1979).

In many schools, however, undergraduates are not permitted to be involved in the grading process. Undergraduates may still be used to provide personalized feedback on work that has already been graded. It should be noted that personalized comments have been shown to result in improved test performance even if they are made on objective tests. Evans and Peeler (1979) conducted a clever experiment in which half of the students in their introductory psychology class were randomly assigned to receive encouraging comments on their objective tests, such as "Excellent job" (for an A) or "It was a hard test. Keep on truckin'" (for a D). The remaining students received no feedback. Students who were randomly assigned to receive feedback scored higher on subsequent tests than students who did not. Hence, undergraduate TAs might be asked to make such personalized comments on the objective tests taken by students in their section.

One particularly successful way that we have used undergraduates in providing personal feedback is by having them make comments on student journals. Students in my introductory psychology classes are typically required to keep a journal. They are asked to pick a topic that reflects some area of their life they would like to change. They are then instructed to apply concepts covered in the course to their problem and to make at least one journal entry per week summarizing their efforts. Each week, the journal is submitted to their undergraduate discussion leader, who in turn provides personalized feedback on their insights, progress, and so forth. This process continues throughout the entire semester.

In most cases, keeping a journal has been rated as the single most valuable aspect of the introductory psychology course. In addition to reporting this to be a worthwhile experience, many students indicated that they had successfully changed their behavior in a way that was highly significant to them. Some recent examples of change include quitting smoking, losing weight, and seeking professional help for a serious mental health problem.

Several articles have appeared in the literature extolling the virtues of journal writing in introductory psychology classes (see Fulwiler, 1987, for a review). As one writer has noted, however, the major disadvantage of using journals is that it is extremely time-consuming to provide written feedback if the class is large (Hettich, 1990). On the basis of our experience, the use of undergraduate assistants would seem to be an ideal solution to this problem. Because journals do not have to be graded, undergraduate TAs can be asked to make comments even at those schools that prohibit undergraduates from involvement in grading.

MINICOURSES

Of all the ways that we have involved undergraduate assistants in the introductory psychology course, perhaps the most successful has been allowing them to offer independent seminars that we call minicourses. Minicourses are short specialty courses taught by the undergraduate TAs on a topic of their choosing. Students from the introductory psychology course are invited to sign up for and attend one or more minicourses during the semester. Each minicourse is limited to 10-15 participants to maximize the personal and interactive nature of this experience. Although there is certainly some flexibility, minicourses generally meet for 1–4 hours spread over 1–4 course meetings.

Early in the semester, undergraduate TAs are instructed to select a topic for their minicourse and to begin looking for interesting reading materials. It is emphasized that the topic selected can be either broad (e.g., mental illness) or narrow (e.g., biofeedback). Each week the undergraduate assistant is required to hand in a tentative syllabus in which topics to be covered, proposed readings, and plans for the use of class time are described. Weekly meetings provide a forum wherein students can receive feedback from the teacher and their peers on how their minicourse can be improved. In these meetings, students are encouraged to design sessions that take advantage of the small class size by actively involving students in the material (e.g., visiting a home for autistic children as part of a minicourse on autism). They are discouraged from lecturing to their students. Students are required to submit refined and improved syllabi each week until it is time for the minicourses to begin.

Minicourses have been offered on a wide variety of topics. Some of the most popular have been on depression, eating disorders, meditation, smoking cessation, hypnosis, AIDS awareness and prevention, family and domestic issues, cultural differences in behavior, the psychology of religion, and sexual assault. If two or more undergraduate assistants want to offer minicourses on the same topic, no attempt is made to dissuade them. It was reasoned that if a topic is popular among the undergraduate assistants, it well be popular among the introductory psychology students as well.

Although students are advised against requesting departmental faculty to appear in their seminars, we encourage the undergraduates to consult with faculty and graduate students for advice about their topic. In our experience faculty members and graduate students have been very helpful when approached in this way. They have often gone out of their way to help the undergraduate assistants procure books, articles, or films. Apparently, the context in which faculty and graduate students were sought out—to provide advice in their area of specialty—was one that they found acceptable and in many cases enjoyable.

Every time we have used the minicourse option as part of the introductory psychology course, we have been impressed by the creativity and imagination TAs have shown in planning class activities, bringing in experts, and arranging educational trips for students. For example, an ex-offender was invited to attend one class in a minicourse on the psychology of imprisonment. He not only discussed life in contemporary prisons but also had a unique perspective on the problems faced by ex-offenders seeking employment. The leader of a minicourse on mental illness arranged a bus trip to a nearby state hospital, where the students had the opportunity to observe inmates in a variety of situations. The leader for a seminar on animal training and behavior took her students to an aquarium for a demonstration of how fish are trained as performers.

After trying various structural arrangements, we have found that it works best to permit each TA to offer his or her minicourse twice. It is extremely valuable for the TAs to have the opportunity to modify their minicourse and try it again on a second group. Having the minicourses offered twice also has the advantage of allowing each introductory psychology student to take two minicourses—an option they find highly desirable.

Each time the minicourse has been included in an introductory psychology class, it has been enormously successful (for a more detailed discussion of the results of an evaluation, see Wortman & Hillis, 1976). Both the introductory psychology students and the undergraduate TAs rate their experiences very highly. For example, on a 5-point scale with endpoints of 1 (*strongly disagree*) and 5 (*strongly agree*), the introductory psychology students expressed clear agreement with the statement that "the leader did a good job of organizing and planning the minicourse" (the main score of 519 students was 4.25). Students also expressed strong agreement with statements that the leader communicated ideas effectively, that he or she was genuinely interested in helping students, that the grading was fair, and that the readings were worthwhile. Students expressed strong disagreement with the statement that the minicourse would have been more effective with a faculty leader.

The undergraduate TAs also appeared to benefit from planning and offering a minicourse. On a 1 (*strongly disagree*) to 5 (*strongly agree*) scale, the mean rating of 33 TAs one term was 4.48 for the item "How valuable an experience was it for you to prepare and teach a minicourse?" The experience of offering a minicourse did not always have the effect of enhancing students' enthusiasm for a career in teaching. Some students were disillusioned by the amount of busywork involved in teaching and by the fact that students seemed concerned only about grades. Others found the experience of providing an intellectual climate exhilarating and could not wait for an opportunity to be in a teaching role again. Virtually all students were glad to have had the exposure to a teaching role and felt better prepared to make job and career decisions that might involve teaching.

RECRUITMENT OF UNDERGRADUATE TEACHING ASSISTANTS

I usually recruit undergraduate TAs by circulating a flyer in upper-division classes. The flyer provides information about what is required of a TA, and it is attached to a one-page application form. The form asks students why they want to be a TA and also requests information about their undergraduate and psychology grade point average and their areas of interest and expertise. Students are asked to provide the names of at least two faculty members who can serve as references.

The course description sheet indicates that only highly qualified students who are recommended by their professors can be selected for the undergraduate teacher role. Hence, applicants probably screen themselves, knowing that those who do not meet strict criteria will not be selected. Perhaps this is why I have rarely had to turn down students who express interest in the position. I typically interview each applicant and ask my colleagues about applicants I do not know. In most cases, the vast majority of students who apply to serve as TAs are selected.

Evaluation of Undergraduate Teaching Assistants

Because the use of undergraduate TAs is somewhat controversial, it is important that such teaching experiences be evaluated. In an educational climate where parents often complain if their son or daughter has too many classes taught by graduate students, what will parental reaction be to undergraduate teaching? Moreover, parents who are devoting significant resources to sending their children to college may not be pleased to learn that (possibly in exchange for course credit) they are spending time grading papers and leading discussions. Concerns of this sort might make deans and department chairpersons uncomfortable about the involvement of undergraduates in teaching introductory psychology. Hence, it is of paramount importance to determine whether the use of undergraduate TAs benefits students enrolled in introductory psychology classes and whether this arrangement is beneficial to the undergraduate TAs themselves.

A number of studies have compared introductory psychology students' reactions to undergraduate and graduate student discussion leaders. For example, White and Kolber (1978) compared the performance of graduate and undergraduate TAs in their introductory course at a private metropolitan university. Students were asked to indicate the extent to which the TA clarified lectures, encouraged discussion, helped skill development, facilitated the examination of psychological concepts, and facilitated the application of such concepts. In each case, there was a highly significant difference between ratings of the graduate and undergraduate TAs, and in each case, these difference favored the *undergraduate* TA. (The authors speculate that the closeness in age between the undergraduate TAs and the introductory psychology students may have had a positive influence on the students' experience with the undergraduate assistants.) In another study (Fremouw, Millard, & Donahoe, 1979), undergraduate TAs were rated as being equally knowledgeable as graduate student assistants and as significantly more helpful than graduate students.

In addition to the other benefits that are conferred, our evaluations suggest that students benefit considerably from regular contact with a small group of undergraduates. Such contact may facilitate integration, particularly for those students who are not gregarious by nature and who may be experiencing some difficulty becoming acquainted with other students. Students also seem to value the opportunity to get to know a junior or senior psychology major who can provide information about such matters as which courses to take and which instructors are most approachable for independent study.

There is also substantial evidence to suggest that the TAs benefit from their involvement in the introductory course. In the evaluation we conducted (Wortman & Hillis, 1976), undergraduate TAs were asked to indicate whether they were glad they had served as TAs. On a scale ranging from 1 (*not at all glad*) to 5 (*extremely glad*), the mean rating made by the 33 TAs was 4.76. In another study, Fremouw et al. (1979) reported that students who served as undergraduate TAs displayed greater knowledge of information presented in an introductory course than did comparable undergraduate controls. Taken together, these studies provide compelling evidence that serving as a TA can be an extremely valuable experience. Along similar lines, undergraduate TAs rated themselves as significantly less anxious in subsequent group situations (Boeding & Vattano, 1976).

Two additional advantages of serving as an undergraduate TA should be noted. One that may be obvious is that students have an opportunity to work closely with a faculty mentor. This often results in a strong and enthusiastic letter of recommendation. Second, the experience of serving as a TA places students in a peer group of highly motivated psychology majors. Students are able to exchange information about such topics as where to apply to graduate school, how to tackle a personal statement, and how to study for Graduate Record Exams.

It should be noted that some schools may have policies or philosophies that make it difficult to integrate the use of undergraduate TAs. In situations like this, it may be possible to utilize only certain portions of this approach. Each portion of this approach (utilizing selected undergraduates to lead discussion sections, provide evaluative feedback, or teach minicourses) can add to an introductory psychology course on its own. For example, advanced undergraduates may be recruited to teach a minicourse, exceptional introductory psychology students may be asked to return the next semester and lead a discussion section, and so forth.

Although some schools or departments may oppose the use of undergraduate TAs in principle, we believe this is unfortunate. Such a policy is often based on a commitment to the highest standards of undergraduate education. In our judgment, whether the use of undergraduate TAs facilitates or impedes the education of introductory psychology students, and of the TAs themselves, is an empirical question. The research evidence in support of this innovation is extremely compelling. Virtually every study to address the matter has documented the extraordinary effectiveness of this approach in enhancing the value of the introductory psychology course for both students and the TAs.

Conclusion

The two teaching techniques reviewed in this chapter—teaching what you are passionate about and using undergraduate TAs—were successful in transforming the teaching of introductory psychology from something dreaded to an exhilarating experience. Within a year, the course was so popular at my university that a lottery had to be instituted to determine who would be permitted to register.

I believe that this format results in higher quality lectures, in part because instructors lecture about things they know and care about and in part because they can devote more time to each lecture. Using the undergraduates as discussion and minicourse leaders creates a win–win situation wherein both introductory students and TAs appear to benefit considerably. The minicourse option provides a unique opportunity to customize the course and hence meet the needs of a diverse body of students. Some students have described our minicourse registration process as "like being a kid in a candy store." Overall, offering the course this way generates a great deal of enthusiasm and excitement.

I'll admit that my goals in offering this course go beyond creating an intellectual milieu that is engaging to the students. What I really want to do is to change students' lives. I believe that for many students, this kind of course can serve as a catalyst for positive change. The last time I lectured about depression, at least five students showed up during office hours stating that they wanted help, and the appropriate calls were made to initiate treatment. A few weeks after lecturing about conflict resolution, I received a visit from a student who indicated that she had drawn on the material to reestablish a relationship with her estranged mother. About a year after the last time I taught introductory psychology, I was contacted by a student who wanted to let me know that she had ended a relationship with her abusive boyfriend. Although incidents of this sort are certainly not conclusive, they suggest that this type of course has the potential to make a difference in students' lives.

Taken together, the options described in this chapter allow for a level of active involvement and personal attention that is unusual in a large introductory psychology course. Moreover, these changes can have the impact of improving the quality of the course without placing additional burdens on the instructor. Perhaps the most compelling reason to consider incorporating these changes, however, is that they provide an experience for the instructor that is particularly gratifying and rewarding.

References

Bernstein, D. J. (1979). Reliability and fairness of grading in a mastery program. *Teaching of Psychology, 6,* 104–107.

Boeding, C. H., & Vattano, F. J. (1976). Undergraduates as teaching assistants: A comparison of two discussion methods. *Teaching of Psychology, 3,* 55–59.

Candland, D. K. (1982). Selective pressure and the teaching of psychology: The fox and the hedgehog. *Teaching of Psychology, 9,* 23–26.

Diamond, M. J. (1972). Improving the undergraduate lecture class by use of student-led discussion groups. *American Psychologist, 27,* 978–981.

Evans, J. D., & Peeler, L. (1979). Personalized comments on returned tests improve test performance in introductory psychology. *Teaching of Psychology, 6,* 57.

Fremouw, W. J., Millard, W. J., & Donahoe J. W. (1979). Learning-through-teaching: Knowledge changes in undergraduate teaching assistants. *Teaching of Psychology, 6,* 30–32.

Fulwiler, T. (Ed.). (1987). *The journal book.* Portsmouth, NH: Boynton/Cook.

Griggs, R. A., Lange, S. K., & Meyer, M. E. (1988). Staffing the introductory psychology course in graduate departments. *Teaching of Psychology, 15,* 124–127.

Hettich, P. (1990). Journal writing: Old fare or nouvelle cuisine? *Teaching of Psychology, 17,* 36–39.

Hubbard, R. W., & McIntosh, J. L. (1992). Integrating suicidology into abnormal psychology classes: The Revised Facts on Suicide Quiz. *Teaching of Psychology, 19,* 163–166.

Koss, M. P., Gidycz, C. A., & Wisniewski, N. (1987). The scope of rape: Incidence and prevalence of sexual aggression and victimization in a national sample of higher education students. *Journal of Consulting and Clinical Psychology, 55,* 162–170.

Lehman, C. R., Ellard, J. H., & Wortman, C. B. (1986). Social support for the bereaved: Recipients' and providers' perspectives on what is helpful. *Journal of Consulting and Clinical Psychology, 54,* 438–446.

Maas, J. B., & Pressler, V. M. (1973, March). The role of undergraduate teaching assistants in introductory psychology. *Teaching of Psychology Newsletter,* pp. 7–9.

McKeachie, W. J. (1986). *Teaching tips: A guidebook for the beginning college teacher* (8th ed.). Lexington, MA: Heath.

McKeachie, W. J. (1987). Teaching, teaching teaching, and research on teaching. *Teaching of Psychology, 14,* 135–139.

Ross, A. S., Anderson, R., & Gaulton, R. (1987). Methods of teaching introductory psychology: A Canadian survey. *Canadian Psychology, 28,* 266–273.

Silver, R. L., Boon, C., & Stones, M. H. (1983). Searching for meaning in misfortune: Making sense of incest. *Journal of Social Issues, 39,* 81–102.

Wallerstein, N. S. (1987). Children after divorce: Wounds that don't heal. *Perspectives in Pediatric Care, 24,* 107–113.

Wallerstein, N. S. (1991). The long-term effects of divorce on children: A review. *Journal of the American Academy of Child and Adolescent Psychiatry, 30,* 349–360.

White, K. M., & Kolber, R. G. (1978). Undergraduate and graduate students as discussion section leaders. *Teaching of Psychology, 5,* 6–9.

Wortman, C. B., & Hillis, J. W. (1976). Undergraduate-taught "mini-courses" in conjunction with an introductory lecture course. *Teaching of Psychology, 3,* 69–72.

Wortman, C. B., & Silver, R. C. (1989). The myths of coping with loss. *Journal of Consulting and Clinical Psychology, 57,* 349–357.

Zanich, M. L., & Grover, D. E. (1989). Introductory psychology from the standpoint of the consumer. *Teaching of Psychology, 16,* 72–75.

Charles L. Brewer

Epilogue

As Richard Griggs's prologue to this volume suggests, teaching introductory psychology is challenging, demanding, exciting, frustrating, rewarding, and fun. In planning and teaching this course, instructors must make important decisions about philosophy, perspectives, general goals, specific objectives, breadth and depth of coverage, topical organization, and the purpose of lectures and related class activities, as well as the use of other pedagogical methods and techniques. The textbook one chooses for the course reflects decisions on these and other similar matters. Writing a textbook is one form of teaching, even if most students who learn from what you write never come to a class you teach. Hence, authors must make critical decisions about these same issues—and many more—when planning and writing an introductory psychology textbook. The book one writes evinces answers to these and many other important questions. Indeed, a textbook may provide its author's definitive answers to all of these questions. Reading what the prominent authors represented in this volume say about how their positions on these and kindred issues influence their teaching of and writing textbooks for the introductory psychology course is informative, provocative, enjoyable, and reassuring.

The authors provide reflective and fascinating accounts of individual odysseys that shaped how they teach introductory psychology and how they write about it for beginning students. Their narratives contain notable and instructive similarities that provide valuable insights for any psychology teacher. In this epilogue, I mention several commonalities that strike me as interesting and important.

A few of these authors admitted that they became psychologists in spite of their own first undergraduate psychology courses. One author said that the course was dreadfully boring because the lectures included an endless recitation of unconnected facts and research findings. Another author said that the teaching was so poor and the textbook so boring that he changed his major to sociology and anthropology because he had come to hate psychology. Luckily, he returned to the fold after taking an exciting course in experimental psychology during his senior year. I wonder how many people become teachers because they want to teach better than they were taught. Is boredom intrinsic or extrinsic motivation?

Several authors were dismayed that they received no training—formal or informal—in how to teach and no supervision when they started teaching. As in most large universities, their graduate programs stressed research, and teaching took a back seat. One notable exception was the author who, after taking Claude Buxton's course (The Teaching of Psychology) felt well prepared and was eager to become the first psychology graduate student at Yale to teach the introductory course. Lamentably, preparing graduate students to be teachers is still a low priority (Benassi & Fernald, 1993; Lumsden, Grosslight, Loveland, & Williams, 1988). Plotnik's commitment and approach to changing the situation at San Diego State University are laudable. But, like Buxton (1951) so long ago, Plotnik still longs for the day when teaching will be raised to the same level as research on psychology's totem pole of values. (See Fernald, 1995, for a description of the University of New Hampshire's commendable program for preparing graduate students to be college teachers.)

A few authors reported writing their introductory textbook because they were dissatisfied with available books. They had a vision of a distinctive book that would be better for their own teaching than other books on the market. After describing the ideal textbook to a psychology editor, one author was told that there was no such book, and the editor challenged him to write one. He did! The ninth edition was published in 1996.

Common themes also emerge from these authors' comments on how they teach and write about introductory psychology. These themes reveal core commitments about our discipline and how it is presented to beginning students.

All of these authors portray psychology as an empirical science that produces broad and tentative knowledge. I wonder who considers psychology to be unscientific, narrow, and immutable. They all strive to keep their courses and textbooks current and exciting. In doing so, they demonstrate what Zimbardo calls an insatiable curiosity, and they try to instill in their students and readers what Matlin and Myers call a sense of wonder.

All of these authors' courses and textbooks reflect the staggering breadth and diversity of psychology, so their coverage must be selective. As Bernstein suggested, "we are forced to lie to introductory psychology students because we don't have time to tell them the truth" (p. 42). I wonder how many teachers have similar reactions about all of their courses.

One overarching goal of all of these authors is to encourage students to think the way scientific psychologists think. Consistent with Dewey's (1933) emphasis and more recent widespread interest among educators, these authors stress active learning and critical thinking in their teaching and writing. (See Halpern & Nummedal, 1995, for an excellent review of how "Psychologists Teach Critical Thinking.") Their chapters in this volume include numerous demonstrations, techniques, and writing assignments designed to promote active learning and critical thinking, especially in large lecture classes. As Sternberg emphasized, thinking should be fully infused into instruction at all times and not just tacked on as an afterthought. Sternberg, Gray, and Wade provide impressive prototypes.

These authors also focus on the "big picture" instead of presenting psychology as an endless collection of isolated facts to be memorized for the next examination. Facts fade fast, and these authors prefer to stress concepts and general principles in their teaching and writing. Despite the fractionation produced by increased specialization in our field, these authors try to present psychology as a unified discipline. Some do so by highlighting the methodology that underlies and transcends psychology's numerous subspecialties. They emphasize the research enterprise rather than the multitudinous research findings that the enterprise has produced.

Another dominant theme concerns these authors' efforts to relate psychology to students' everyday lives. Several specifically mentioned Miller's (1969) famous exhortation about giving psychology away. While recognizing that students should understand the practical relevance of psychology, we must be vigilant in presenting the rigorous scientific underpinnings that distinguish psychology from more speculative modes of inquiry. Otherwise, there will be nothing left in psychology that is worth having, much less giving away. Lefton and I agree with Morris, who said, "Trying to be all things to all people in a single course is no small challenge—there is always the danger that one will end up being nothing to anybody" (p. 92). Frankly, I hope that we never give all of psychology away.

As writers and teachers, these authors use findings from psychological research to improve their pedagogy. In many cases, presentations of material in their textbooks and classes reflect what we know about enhancing learning and memory. Hence, these authors practice what they preach when they write and teach.

Another important aim of these authors, explicit and implicit, is to dispel misimpressions and challenge students' misconceptions. (Jostling a few folkways, without being audacious or judgmental, is probably an admirable goal for all teachers.) In the process, they try to simplify without oversimplifying, and they emphasize that we and our students must learn to tolerate uncertainty but try to decrease it whenever we can.

Consistent with a noticeable trend (see Furumoto, 1989), these authors recognize that psychology develops and must be understood in a sociocultural context. While stressing that psychology influences and is affected by multicultural milieus, these authors celebrate all aspects of diversity within and among different groups.

Underlying all of these commonalities are two other themes that I consider preeminent. First, several authors comment on passion as the paramount ingredient for successful teaching and writing—and for sustaining enthusiasm for both. Without passion, these authors—and, I would say, all teachers—would be less successful than they are. I admire and salute their passion for passion! Second, this passion leads to an intense desire to make a difference in students' lives in the long run. After the facts fade, as they surely will, what impact will introductory psychology and its teachers have? All of these authors would probably agree with Henry Adams's suggestion that teachers affect eternity; they never know where their influence stops. A few of them address this issue directly. Wortman and Smyth say, "What I really want to do is to change students' lives" (p. 178), and Zimbardo concludes, "I want to make a significant difference in the lives of as many of my students as possible" (p. 14). The real reason for teaching is to make a difference—to be important to someone. These authors are good teachers because they stretch the heart as well as the mind. Their humaneness is transparent, sincere, and unpretentious.

Finally, I am struck by how similar these common themes are to many of the observations and recommendations from the American Psychological Association's National Conference on Enhancing the Quality of Undergraduate Education in Psychology, which was held at St. Mary's College of Maryland in June 1991 (McGovern, 1993). These similarities indicate not only that these outstanding authors are au courant but also that they understand the historical development of undergraduate psychology curricula (cf. Lloyd & Brewer, 1992; McGovern, 1992). Introductory psychology will continue to flourish as long as these unusual psychologists teach it and write about it. I will be a better teacher after being challenged by these authors to think more deeply and analytically about teaching and how to do it. In this case at least, T. S. Eliot was right: "The end is where we start from."

References

Benassi, V. A., & Fernald, P. S. (1993). Preparing tomorrow's psychologists for careers in academe. *Teaching of Psychology, 20,* 149–155.

Buxton, C. E. (1951). Teaching: Have your cake and eat it too? *American Psychologist, 6,* 111–118.

Dewey, J. (1933). *How we think: A restatement of the relation of reflective thinking to the educative process.* Boston: Heath.

Fernald, P. S. (1995). Preparing psychology graduate students for the professoriate. *American Psychologist, 50,* 421–427.

Furumoto, L. (1989). The new history of psychology. In I. S. Cohen (Ed.), *The G. Stanley Hall Lecture Series* (Vol. 9, pp. 5–34). Washington, DC: American Psychological Association.

Halpern, D. F., & Nummedal, S. G. (1995). Psychologists teach critical thinking [Special issue]. *Teaching of Psychology, 22*(1).

Lloyd, M. A., & Brewer, C. L. (1992). National conferences on undergraduate psychology. In A. E. Puente, J. R. Matthews, & C. L. Brewer (Eds.), *Teaching psychology in America: A history* (pp. 263–284). Washington, DC: American Psychological Association.

Lumsden, E. A., Grosslight, J. H., Loveland, E. H., & Williams, J. E. (1988). Preparation of graduate students as classroom teachers and supervisors in applied and research settings. *Teaching of Psychology, 15,* 5–9.

McGovern, T. V. (1992). Evolution of undergraduate curricula in psychology, 1892–1992. In A. E. Puente, J. R. Matthews, & C. L. Brewer (Eds.), *Teaching psychology in America: A history* (pp. 13–38). Washington, DC: American Psychological Association.

McGovern, T. V. (1993). (Ed.). *Handbook for enhancing undergraduate education in psychology.* Washington, DC: American Psychological Association.

Miller, G. A. (1969). Psychology as a means of promoting human welfare. *American Psychologist, 24,* 1063–1075.

Index

About the Editor

Robert J. Sternberg, PhD, is IBM Professor of Psychology and Education in the Department of Psychology at Yale University. Dr. Sternberg is the author of two introductory psychology texts, *In Search of the Human Mind* and *Pathways to Psychology*, as well as the text *Cognitive Psychology*, and has made the teaching of introductory psychology one of his areas of research. His research on the teaching of psychology has aimed to incorporate the triarchic theory of intelligence, the investment theory of creativity, and the mental self-government theory of thinking styles to promote learning and thinking in psychology. The author of about 600 books and journal articles, Dr. Sternberg is a fellow of the American Psychological Association, the American Psychological Society, the American Academy of Arts and Sciences, and the American Association for the Advancement of Science.